INTENTIONAL LEADERSHIP

The Glen's Market Culture

Glen A. Catt

ISBN 978-1-63630-574-5 (Paperback)
ISBN 978-1-63885-604-7 (Hardcover)
ISBN 978-1-63630-575-2 (Digital)

Covenant Books, Inc.
11661 Hwy 707
Murrells Inlet, SC 29576
www.covenantbooks.com

This book is dedicated to C. Glen Catt (1925–1996)
and
Norberta "Bert" Woloszyk (1943–1994)

Glen's MARKETS

*"People working with People,
Serving People"*

Mission

... To operate supermarkets in an ethical manner that provides the greatest possible customer value while earning a fair profit that will ensure security for our company and associates.

Belief

... To adhere to The Golden Rule in all our relationships with customers, associates suppliers and our communities.

Objectives

... **Customer Relations:** To always treat our customers as guests.

... **Value:** To offer the best combination of quality, variety, service and price.

... **Image:** To maintain our reputation of cleanliness and friendliness.

... **Associates:** To hire individuals of moral character and provide an environment where personal development and open communication is encouraged.

... **Culture:** To recognize and respect each associate as a valued member of our family.

... **Community Involvement:** To be involved in building a better community together.

... **Environment:** To do our part in conserving our natural resources.

... **Business Plan:** To obtain optimum market share and operating results that enables us to meet, or exceed, our budgeted expectations.

... **Financial:** To provide continued financial security for our company and associates.

CHAPTER 1

The Glen's History

The integrity of the upright will guide them, but the crookedness of the treacherous will destroy them.

—Proverbs 11:3

C. Glen Catt, December 18, 1025–March 30, 1996

C. Glen Catt 1925–1996

Orrie Glen and Rula Fay Catt had two sons, Robert Keith Catt and Charles Glen Catt. Upon having visitors for their first child and people commenting how cute that was to have a son, Bob Catt, Orrie and Rula immediately started calling Robert by his middle name, Keith. Two years later, when Charles came along, visitors started calling him Charlie. Rula had sour feelings about Orrie's father (also named Charlie) so they started calling him by his middle name, Glen.

Orrie's father, Charlie Catt, had come to America from Sussex, England, when he was three years old, arriving in New York, New York, March 19, 1858. A year later, his parents moved to Barry, Michigan. Orrie was born August 22, 1899. Rula came from a broken home and thus grew up living with different families most of her adolescent years. Her paternal father was the Reverend Claude Sylvester Houk; however, we could never get Grandma to talk about him. There was a bad history there too, in fact so much that she assumed the maiden name for the woman whose home she last lived in. And that was of Estelle Ferguson Catt, Orrie's mother. Her last residence was with Charlie and Estelle Catt, hence how she met Orrie, but still she didn't think much of my great-grandfather, Charlie.

The Catts were a poor but a humble family. Grandpa (always referred to as Pop) said the depression didn't bother them much because they didn't have much to lose, compounding that with the limited job market, they struggled but persevered. After years of not having full-time employment, Orrie was eventually hired by a firm that had a contract to build US 131, the state road that would eventually connect Ohio to Mackinaw City, Michigan, the point where Lake Huron and Lake Michigan connect. The company, however, eventually went bankrupt during construction of the road near Kalkaska, so Pop was able get a job driving a road grader for Kalkaska County, Rula got a job as a cashier at the local Kroger, while Keith and Glen, still in school, got part-time jobs delivering advertising house-to-house for the Kroger store.

Orrie G. Catt 1900–1978 (circled) Kalkaska
County Maintenance Crew about 1945

C. Glen Catt left high school early and joined the U.S. Air Force
during the Korean War. He was a tail gunner in a B-26. When he
returned to Kalkaska, he obtained his High School Diploma

Growing up in this atmosphere, Dad shared that he was determined to find work that would hold security for his family, hoping they would never want for where their next meal would come from. He figured that people had to eat; thus, he decided that the grocery business was a good bet. So when he was old enough, he worked at the little Kroger. During that time, he met a gal working in the S.S. Kresge 5&10 Store next door (for those not familiar with Kresge's 5&10s, they were the beginning of the later-to-come K-marts, etc.). It wasn't long after that C. Glen Catt and Doris J. McDonald were married. After serving his country in the Korean War, Glen returned to the Kroger in Kalkaska. Shortly after, he was transferred to Paw Paw, Michigan, in the southwest part of Michigan. This is where I was born. Kroger had promoted him to the position of a store manager there. Within a year or so, Felpausch Foods, a small, family-owned group of stores, offered Dad the position of being a store manager in a new store that they were going to build in Parchment, just north of Kalamazoo. Being the store manager of a new, more modern grocery store seemed very appealing to Dad although his long-term goal was to own his stores at some point.

However, for whatever reason, that new store never developed or possibly got delayed. Nevertheless, I remember Dad saying that the combination of personalities of the store manager that he was working for and the manager's wife, the front-end manager (who sounded like she felt she was the store manager) created a culture that was not enjoyable for him to work in. Hence, he decided to leave.

At the same time, his family back in Kalkaska said that Kroger had announced that it was going to close. This would have been about the time that Kroger was starting to eliminate its smaller, less profitable stores. At the time, they had over 5,500 little stores around the country, where now, seventy-plus years later, Kroger lists about half that many but large supermarkets. Thus, Dad made the long (in those days) 185-mile drive back to Kalkaska to negotiate a lease with the local individual who owned the 2,000-square-foot building that Kroger would be vacating, sealing it with a handshake. Dad returned to Felpausch, gave his notice, raised $400.00, bought a large trailer load of used equipment, and moved my mom, sister, and myself to

Kalkaska (my brother, Larry, wouldn't have been brought into this world yet).

Arriving in Kalkaska, Dad found out that the landlord had leased the building to the previous store manager, Harry Gosling. (Ironically, years later when I was the store manager of our Kalkaska store and the president of the newly recreated Kalkaska Chamber of Commerce, I hired Harry to be the chamber director after he had decided to close his store and retire.) Being without a job and borrowed to the max, Dad started looking around northern Michigan for a location that he could pursue to fill his dream.

In Gaylord, about 40 miles northeast of Kalkaska, he found a 2,500-square-foot vacant grocery store that hadn't been closed too long. The building was still owned by the prior proprietor, Mr. Vincent. I don't ever remember meeting Mr. Vincent, but I know enough of the story that he was a one-armed man, who hadn't been successful with his business so he closed and moved back to East Jordan, about 35 miles northwest of Gaylord. Although locals said Mr. Vincent was unsuccessful because the business was *on the wrong side of the tracks*, creating a physiological barrier, Dad felt it was a good location (actually, he didn't have many options at the time) and chose to lease the building with an option to purchase, which he exercised a couple of years later.

On June 7, 1951, Glen's Market opened its first doors to what would become a legacy in itself.

First Glen's Market opened June 7, 1951

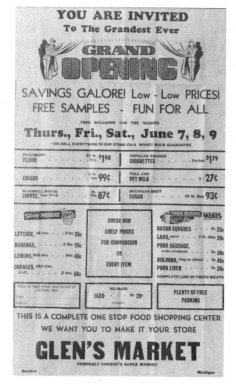

Opening advertisement

The early Glen's Market logo, displayed here
on a Glen's bowling team jacket

THREE GLENS were captured in this family photo: Glen B. Catt sits on the lap of grandmother Rula Catt, while his father Glen A. Catt (middle) and grandfather, C. Glen Catt, Glen's founder.

4 generations L-R Rula Catt, Glen B. Catt,
Glen A. Catt, C. Glen Catt

"Mom", "Pop", and C. Glen at the snack bar in Glen's—1969

C. Glen Catt with his children Larry D. Catt,
Sandy Freeman, and Glen A. Catt

New replacement Glen's to the right of the original Glen's 1954

Dad next to produce case in new Gaylord store 1954

Mom Catt at one of the two registers 1954

Employees in front of the new Glen's Market—1954; L-R Larry Northey (high school but years later meat manager), Mom (Rula) Catt, unknown, unknown, Doris J. Catt (1924–2012), Ed Kuras (later became the store manager), Bob Warner (high school but years later store manager), Irene Koronka (became head cashier who could speak fluent Polish), unknown, Pop (Orrie) Catt, and Sam Northey (meat manager but later meat supervisor).

Glen's Market Chronology
1951–1999

1951—June 7, first store in Gaylord opened

1954—New replacement store built in Gaylord

1956—New store opened in Kalkaska

1957—Opened addition built onto Gaylord store

1959—Store purchased in Grayling from another Spartan-supplied retailer

1962—Opened addition built onto Grayling store

1963—Purchased store in East Jordan from another Spartan-supplied retailer

1965—Opened another addition built onto Grayling store

1966—Opened addition built onto the Kalkaska store

1967—Opened new replacement store in Alpine Plaza in Gaylord

1968—Opened new replacement store in East Jordan

1970—Opened new laundry and dry cleaning store in Gaylord

1971—Purchased store in West Branch from an independent retailer

1972—Purchased store in Mio from an independent retailer

Opened new replacement store in West Branch

Opened new replacement store in Mio

Opened new replacement store in Grayling

Opened new addition on Gaylord store

1973—Kalkaska store destroyed by fire

1974—Opened new Kalkaska store at new location

1975—Purchased store in Mancelona from A&P

Purchased store in Roscommon from A&P

1976—Opened new replacement store in Mancelona

1977—Purchased store in Rose City from an independent retailer

Opened addition built onto the Mio store

1978—Opened new store in Charlevoix

Purchased store in Houghton Lake from another Spartan-supplied retailer

1979—Opened new replacement store in East Jordan at a new location

1981—Opened new store in Rogers City

Opened addition built onto Kalkaska store

1982—Opened addition built onto the West Branch store

1983—Opened addition built onto the Gaylord store

1984—Opened new store in Lewiston

Purchased store in Boyne City from another Spartan-supplied retailer

Opened addition built onto Grayling store

1985—Opened expanded office facilities in the Gaylord store building

1986—Purchased store in St. Ignace from independent retailer supplied by wholesaler, Red Owl

Purchased store in Iron Mountain from wholesaler, Red Owl

Purchased store in Munising from wholesaler, Red Owl

Purchased store in Sault Ste. Marie from wholesaler, Red Owl

Purchased newly constructed store in Escanaba from wholesaler, Red Owl

Opened newly built, replacement store in St. Ignace

1987—Opened addition built onto the Sault Ste. Marie store

Opened addition built onto the Charlevoix store

Opened addition built onto the West Branch store

Opened addition built onto the Kalkaska store

1988—Sold Iron Mountain store

Sold Escanaba store

Purchased the Alpine Village Pharmacy from an independent pharmacist

Purchased store in Alpena from another Spartan retailer

1989—Opened addition built onto the Mio store

Remodeled the Mancelona store

Remodeled the Rose City store

1990—Opened addition built onto the Houghton Lake store

Opened new store in Cadillac

Opened new store in Oscoda

Purchased store in Cheboygan from another Spartan-supplied retailer

Added deli/bakery to Kalkaska store

Remodeled the Alpena store

1991—Opened new distribution center in Waters
1992—Opened addition added to the Roscommon store
1993—Completely remodeled Cheboygan store
    Opened new replacement store in Sault Ste. Marie
    Moved Alpine Pharmacy into the Gaylord store
    Opened new Movie Plus in old Alpine Pharmacy location
    Purchased Pic-n-Save store in Cadillac and moved from current
        location in Cadillac
    Purchased second location in Alpena from retailer, Giant
    Purchased location in East Tawas from retailer, Giant
    Purchased location in Petoskey from retailer, Giant
    Purchased fleet of semi-tractors and trailers to start hauling our
        own dry groceries
1994—Opened new replacement store in Munising
    Opened new addition built onto the Grayling store
    Totally remodeled Cadillac store
    Purchased second location in Petoskey from Buy Low and
        totally remodeled
1995—Opened Movie Plus in Grayling
1996—Opened new replacement store in West Branch
    Opened Movie Plus store in West Branch
    Remodeled Alpine Laundry and Dry Cleaning after fire
1997—Sold Movie Plus stores to Horizon Video
    Opened addition to Gaylord store
    Opened Dairy Queen and food court in Gaylord store
    Converted downtown Alpena store to a Save-A-Lot limited
        assortment store
    Opened new addition built onto the Charlevoix store
    Converted East Tawas store to a Save-A-Lot limited assortment
        store
1998—Totally remodeled the Cadillac store
1999—Spartan stores purchased Glen's Market retail operation

CHAPTER 2

The Building of a Foundation

Like a Structure, the Building Can Only Be as Solid as the Foundation that It Was Built On

Where there is no vision, the people are unrestrained.

—Proverbs 29:8

Like other young entrepreneurs, C. Glen (or should I continue with Dad?) worked every day the store was open, seven days a week, always opening and most often closing. Choosing to be known for his service, the store was open 7:00 a.m.–9:00 p.m. Monday through Saturday and 8:00 a.m.–1:00 p.m. and 4:00 p.m.–6:00 p.m. on Sundays. It was his desire for each of the employees (yes, those employed back then were referred to as employees) to be able to have a Sunday afternoon dinner with their family. Likewise, quite often that first year, Sunday afternoon may be the only time that my sister, Sandy, and I would see Dad during the week. Not many years later, for the convenience of the customer, the store was open seven days a week, 7:00 a.m.–9:00 p.m.

By the second year he was open, our mom, Doris, also started working at the store more hours as Sandy (now eight years old) and myself (now five years old) would also be working at the store after school and many times on Saturdays.

You may ask, what can an eight- and a five-year-old be doing in a grocery store? We would be in the produce department. Potatoes would come in fifty-pound bags, so we would sort out any bad ones and repackage the good ones into five- and ten-pound bags (allowing an adult to weigh our guesstimates). Likewise, we would take onions from fifty-pound bags and take the husks off them, along with corn and any other items that the produce manager could give us to keep us busy. We actually thought it was a pretty good deal as we would get to see our dad more, Mom would be there, and they paid us 25 cents an hour. It was only later that we found out that a babysitter was getting 35 cents an hour. I guess Dad needed to get a return on us too. Nevertheless, it resulted in building strong work ethics in both Sandy and myself. Mom continued to be very active in the business until our brother, Larry, came along in 1956, and then she decided to stay home to care for him. By then, Sandy and I were on the schedule like everyone else and, likewise, received a weekly payroll check on Fridays at the minimum wage level—$1.00 an hour at the time. I would have been nine years old, and Sandy would have been twelve. She continued to work in produce, and I would stock shelves and bag groceries.

Also, that second year, after purchasing much of his groceries from Alpena Wholesale, a small regional wholesaler in northern Michigan, and the remaining items from the numerous smaller truck vendors, Dad realized that it was hard to compete with the larger A&P in town. They carried much more variety than he had available, and he didn't have opportunities to purchase as many specials that he could pass on to his customers. In early 1951, when he was first ready to open, he had contacted Spartan Stores Inc. (then known as the Grand Rapids Wholesale Company), located in Grand Rapids, Michigan, and inquired about them serving his store. They told him that his store was too small for them to deliver to, plus it was out of the way to get a truck to him on a regular basis. I remember it very well when our dad told our mom one morning a year later, "Doris, I am packing two white shirts, driving to Grand Rapids, and I am not coming back until Grand Rapids Wholesale agrees to service our store!" At my age, I remember it because it left a fearful memory as to if or when I may see my dad again. At five years old, it's hard to understand that kind of stuff. Well, Dad made it home that night. While he was there, based on his first year's sales, and his determination, not only did they accept him as a new Spartan member, they even put together an order for him that would be delivered later that week. It speaks well of the focus and commitment that Dad had and later instilled in his three children. Little would that small wholesaler in Grand Rapids know, but years later, Dad would serve twenty-five years on their board of directors, becoming the president the last year before he led the board to decide to hire a professional to reside in that position full-time. A number of years later, I would also serve on the Spartan board of directors for ten years. During that time, Glen's Markets would become their second largest customer purchasing over $150 million of product a year from them.

C. Glen's philosophy continued to meet the needs and wants of his customers. Starting with day one, he initiated having the team carry groceries to the customer's cars. This may not have been the first in the industry, but it sure was a first for Gaylord, Michigan.

Another customer service he started was taking an individual's personal check. In northern Michigan, people being able to pay their bills with a piece of paper other than cold, hard cash was fairly new. But for the convenience of the customer, Dad started taking personal checks for the amount of their purchase and then later for amounts over their purchase. No one else in the area was doing it, especially the local A&P of which was Dad's biggest competitor. Soon after, Dad started offering to cash payroll checks. Surely, they weren't the size of payroll checks people receive today, but everything was relevant.

The challenge of taking personal checks and cashing payroll checks caused Dad to not have the cash flow available to pay the various vendors that were delivering products daily. Even after convincing Spartan Stores to be his main supplier, there were still product needs where he had to have smaller vendors deliver. Early on, they wanted cash. Later, after he was able to build his credibility, they accepted a check and even gave him credit for in-between deliveries. He would pay them today for what they delivered last week. However, there were always the beer and wine vendors. According to the laws of the state of Michigan at the time, they had to be paid at delivery (and checks were not an option). With numerous vendors stopping by to deliver product every day, this put Dad in a situation to have to gather up all the checks from his two cash registers and literally trot down to the Gaylord State Bank, one block away, cash them, and then trot back to the store with the cash. However, his "trot" was more of a medium-speed run. This continued for close to two years when a local businessman, Walt Drzewiecki Sr., owner of the local Gaylord Feed and Grain, had Dad over for coffee. Walt's feed and grain was located just kitty corner on the same block. His southwest property touched the store's northeast property; hence, Mr. Drzewiecki seemed to understand the right timing to invite Dad over for a quick cup of joe. Hearing of Dad running back and forth to the bank, Mr. Drzewiecki walked to his safe, returned with a zippered, vinyl bag, and said, "Glen, in here should be enough cash to allow you to stay at your store and just go to the bank late in the day. You can just pay me back when you get the funds." Many years later, when Mr. Drzewiecki was celebrating fifty years in business, I was able to stop by with a plaque, which I had a business make, of the local paper's announcement of their fifty years, and with it, I repeated the story that Dad had told so often. As I shared the details as I remembered them, Mr. Drzewiecki sat there with a large smile on his face while his oldest son Wally listened intently. As it was, that was the kind of support that Dad continued to receive from numerous businessmen in the community because of the respect that he had been building from the integrity of his nature.

At the time, we were living in a small two-room apartment above the Gaylord State Bank. One of the local dentists, Dr. Donick, stopped my dad on the street and said, "Glen, with all the hours you are working, you need to get your family into a house." After Dad shared that all their cash flow had to be reinvested into the store, the good doctor reached into his sport coat, pulled out a checkbook, wrote a check, and said, "Glen, this should cover a down payment on any house in Gaylord. Just pay me back when you can." Needless to say, we then moved into 308 E. Petoskey Street, and Dad just worked all the harder so he could pay the good doctor back. We lived in that home until I was a junior in high school.

Another policy Dad instilled was no questions asked when a customer had a return or a perceived, negative experience. I remember Dottie Snook sharing a story with me. Dottie and Fred Snook had just moved to town to open up a small sporting goods shop on Main Street. Their sons were young, and being a Sunday, there weren't many stores open. The kids needed some sweatshirts and various clothes, which Glen's Market carried as part of trying to cover everyone's needs/wants. Dottie told me, "I went into your dad's store and bought my groceries and a couple of sets of warmer clothes for the kids, Fred, and me. When I got home and started unpacking the non-grocery items, I realized that I was missing two to three bags of my purchases. In the move north, cash was short, and I was terrified of going back to the store and telling someone that I didn't get everything. I immediately went back, and when I shared my situation with a cashier, she called someone up front and told them to help Mrs. Snook pick up everything that she could remember that she didn't have when she got home. There were no questions asked. You know, Glen, that was over thirty years ago, and I have never shopped at another grocery store in Gaylord since then."

Early on, Dad realized that Gaylord housed a very large number of Polish ancestors, many of whom could not speak English or at least clear English. Hiring a young twenty-year-old gal, Irene Koronka, who was fluent in English and Polish, he placed her at one of the checkouts during the busiest times of the week. With the Catholic Church just around the corner, especially on Sundays, Irene's register would be backed up with Polish-speaking customers. Shortly afterward, Dad promoted Irene to the front-end manager's position.

Glen's Markets was the first in the area, later I was told, even in the state, to start hiring high school students to bag groceries and stock shelves. Dad was flexible in working around their school and sports activities (with my sports ability, or should I say lack of, I ended up working each night of a basketball or football game, getting to the games by the later part of the third quarter). This helped the school kids out, gave Dad more flexibility in the schedule, and allowed many of the full-time employees to be at home with their families in the evenings.

Four years after opening the first Glen's Market, Dad's dream became more realized when he had an opportunity to purchase a parcel of land back in his hometown of Kalkaska, Michigan. Although it was half-a-block off Main Street, it would be right next to the US Post Office, a building frequented by most of the town throughout the week. In January 1956, Dad opened his second store.

Ironically, eleven and a half years later, I would become the store manager of that store. During my nine years as the store manager there, we were able to add an addition onto the store, and in August 1973, the Kalkaska store experienced an electrical fire that destroyed the total building (contrary to some suspicions I had not burned the store down so that I could get a new store to manage). As it was, Jeanne and I had been dating, so we took the opportunity to get married between the fire and the new, replacement store opening.

Every associate was offered the opportunity to work in one of our other stores (we had five other stores at the time). Full-time associates would be paid travel expenses. If an associate chose not to travel to another store, they were offered the opportunity to collect unemployment. We even had a number of high school students drive to Grayling to work, a short now, but seemed longer back then, 25 miles.

Advertisement for Glen's second location—Kalkaska
January 19, 1956

Glen's Market, Kalkaska (next to the U.S. Post Office)

Kalkaska Glen's Market after the fire, August 1973

Dad, Jeanne, and me at the Kalkaska
replacement store opening—1974

In 1959, a Spartan member in Grayling placed his store on the market and, after negotiations, became the third location for Dad, fulfilling his hidden goal to someday own three grocery stores. The three stores actually formed a small triangle in the middle of northern Michigan, allowing Dad to spend time in all three on the same day.

In 1963, Denny Freeman, Sandy's new husband, joined the company, and shortly after, a fourth location opened up in East Jordan, with Denny as the store manager, creating an almost four-sided square of locations about 30–40 miles apart. Although Denny was more limited in his experience in the grocery business, he had worked with his father in a feed and grain business in southeast Michigan. What Denny lacked in the grocery business, he quickly made up in associates and customer relations, in short making the new East Jordan location an almost immediate success. After a year, I don't think there was anyone who came through the front door whom Denny didn't know their name, and if he didn't, he was face-to-face within seconds.

I think Dad figured that four stores may be the extent of his growth. But in 1968, Spartan Stores, our main supplier, encouraged him to consider a store in West Branch. While he was doing his due diligence on the town of West Branch, he came across a little town between West Branch and Grayling. Mio actually wasn't even an incorporated town. Legally, it was still considered a settlement. He was more excited about the possibility of building a store in Mio than he was in West Branch, but Spartan was still encouraging him to expand to West Branch. So what did Dad do? He brought in his four store managers (of which I was one); his brother Keith, who had taken a retirement from the Navy to join the company and address the accounting for his brother), and two other individuals who had been working in the offices in supervisory positions at the time, and got us together. He said, "It was always my dream to have three grocery stores, and now we have four. Now, we have an opportunity to open up two more, but this is not something that I wish to go into alone. Together, we are going to look at the locations. If you are interested in doing this together, I will front the finances, but we will start a new corporation with each of you, if you desire, purchasing up to 2 percent, and we will do this together. If you do not have the cash to invest but you desire to, I will loan you the funds, and we can set up a payroll deduction." Thirty-one years later when we sold the grocery business to Spartan Stores, every one of the additional twenty-two locations would have been included in that new corporation that was formed that year. Likewise, at the time of the sale, because we continued to allow leadership to "purchase" stock, fifty-three individuals would profit from the sale of that stock. (Those who were still with the company and still had their 2 percent? It would have now been valued well over seven figures.) Dad always said, "Those who help plan the trip should also enjoy the ride." There is no doubt that having "ownership" changes one's attitude in their work and commitment. An interesting side note of the West Branch/Mio growth in the same year, Spartan Stores had done an intensive market study to come up with the need for another supermarket in the West Branch market, while Dad had drove around Mio and checked the status of the banking institutions in the area (deposits, holdings, etc., as he was familiar from being on the Gaylord bank board of directors then). He made his decision based on his gut and common sense. Although Spartan heavily suggested against the move to Mio, that location actually made a profit the first year and only continued to grow. Meanwhile, the West Branch lost quite a bit of money the first four years, only to barely break even the fifth year of business. This wasn't the last time Dad's common sense assisted him in making key decisions against the tide.

Early picture of those in the Gaylord office/operation: L-R Gale
Parker (started in high school, later became V.P. maintance and
construction), C. Glen Catt, Bert Taylor (would retire as V.P.
meat division), Bill Wishart (Gaylord store manager), Bill Brown
(personel, later became director of personel) Ernie Grocock (general
merchandise supervisor), and R. Keith Catt (later executive V.P.)

Store managers and staff after West Branch and Mio stores were
open; Top L-R Tom Otto (Mio manager) Bert Taylor, Bill Wishart
(Gaylord manager) Dan Tibbe (East Jordan manager), Ernie Grocock,
bottom L-R Del Lewis (West Branch store manager), Denny
Freeman (East Jordan store manager) C. Glen Catt, R. Keith Catt,
Glen A. Catt (Kalkaska store manager... hey, where's my tie?)

C. Glen Catt was not a talker. He was a self-proclaimed intro-vert. He was exposed to numerous people, but few knew him inti-mately. Those who watched him and witnessed his actions had one common term that was most common in discussion behind his back, and that was that he was a man of integrity. I would hear that from customers who knew him, local businesspeople, and each of those who had come into contact with him through the businesses and organizations he was involved in. He was a man of integrity!

Some of his other one-liners, those of us who were close to him, could quote were the following:

> What is right is right. What is wrong is wrong. There is no in-between. (C. Glen Catt)

> Be an example. It is the number one key to suc-cessful leadership. Your actions speak louder than your words. (C. Glen Catt)

> Be firm, but be fair! (C. Glen Catt)

> If you want to be a leader, think like a leader, look like a leader, and act like a leader. (C. Glen Catt)

> What is more important, to be liked or to be respected? (C. Glen Catt)

I was probably seventeen years old when Dad called me into his twelve-foot-by-sixteen-foot plywood-sided office that my grand-father had built in the back room of the (then) old Gaylord store and that he shared with his brother, Keith. Catching a time when he was alone, he asked me this question: "What is more important to you? To be liked? Or to be respected?" I remember saying "Both!" He followed with that not being an option sometimes. My response was something like, "Could I get back to you?" About a week later, I stopped by after watching my uncle walk out and told my dad I had an answer. He said he wondered if I was still thinking about it. I told him, "I sure want to be liked, but given a choice, I would rather people respected me." Dad's response was, "There will be times in your life that you will have to choose between the two. Exceptional leaders make decisions based on what is right, not what others think." (As I came to realize later, if you want to please everyone, you just have to buy them ice cream. Everyone likes ice cream. Otherwise, if you try and please everyone, you will end up not pleasing anyone. You need to put the purpose over the preferences and do what is right for the purpose and the majority.)

> You never have a second chance to make a first impression. (C. Glen Catt)

> Use things not people, love people not things. (C. Glen Catt)

> The phone is my greatest tool. Seek other's opinions, but know that you are still the one who has to make the final decision. (C. Glen Catt)

> You have to spend money to make money. (C. Glen Catt)

However, in light of the preceding quote, he was always quick to say everything has a balance: "Just because you have money doesn't mean you have to spend it" (C. Glen Catt).

As a result of Dad's leading and his example, in the 1980s, we put together the following Glen's Market Mission Statement, from which we strived to live by daily:

THE GLEN'S APPROACH

THIS WE BELIEVE:

OUR COMMITMENT AS A SUPERMARKET BUSINESS:

As a significant link in the food chain, between grower and consumer, it is our responsibility to provide our consumer with an optimum variety of food products and conveniences at a fair value for quality and services rendered.

OUR COMMITMENT TO OUR ASSOCIATES (FAMILY MEMBERS):

We have a special responsibility to our Associates. We desire to create a positive culture of: Opportunities, fair treatment, security, fair and adequate wages, fair and reasonable work hours, acceptable benefits, and systems to share ideas and concerns. These must be the standards by which we operate our company. We must recognize each Associate as an individual, provide proper training, education and coaching, and promote from within whenever possible.

We realize that Associates enjoy a personal life outside of their role with our company. In order for their lives to be in balance, we must constantly strive to improve our culture so that this balance can be obtained.

At Glen's we realize that if we put our Associates first and treat each other in a manner that is deserving of our number one asset, it will naturally follow that our Associates will treat our customers with consideration and respect.

OUR COMMITMENT TO OUR CUSTOMERS (GUESTS):

We realize that without customers, none of us have security in our roles here at Glen's Markets. Serving customers' wants and needs is, and always will be, the only way our company can grow. Proper service leads to satisfied customers, which means more hours and opportunities for all of us.

OUR COMMITMENT TO OUR COMMUNITIES, ENVIRONMENT & GOVERNMENT:

We have the opportunity to touch many lives, and it is our responsibility to do our best to improve the quality of life for those around us. We can do this by working together to make Glen's a model business in each of the communities we serve through personal involvement in community issues and activities.

We can also create an atmosphere in which we not only offer opportunities to help preserve our environment but strive to get others involved; through this effort, generations to come will enjoy the natural beauty and resources of our planet.

It is our responsibility to get involved in local, state and federal government by exercising our vote and our influence in the areas that we believe are best for the majority. One person can make a difference.

OUR COMMITMENT TO OUR SUPPLIERS:

We realize that in order to secure the right product for our customers, it is important that we form partnerships with our suppliers. Although we are our suppliers' customer, in our attempt to obtain the best possible quality at the best possible price, we must maintain an ongoing win/win relationship with each supplier with which we work.

OUR COMMITMENT TO OUR STOCKHOLDERS & INVESTORS:

It is only through making a fair profit and a return on our investment that we will be able to maintain the company we have learned to enjoy - one that continues to grow and prosper. Profit is a necessity for the security of all our Stakeholders.

THIS WE UNDERSTAND:

We understand that consumers, our Associates, our customers, our communities, our environment, our various governments, our suppliers, our stockholders and our investors together constitute our "Stakeholders". Stakeholders are the direct beneficiaries of decisions made by our company. Although Stakeholders, in a way, are equal, we need to prioritize their roles as these relate to the attainment of our goals.

OUR GOALS ARE:

"To accomplish something collectively that we could not accomplish separately. To make a contribution to society while, at the same time, obtaining unselfish goals for ourselves, our families and our future."

With God's help, we will fulfill these opportunities and obligations to the best of our abilities.

The expanded Glen's Mission Statement

C. Glen Catt at retirement

C. Glen Catt Retirement Video

Dennis W. Freeman and Glen A. Catt
at the time we purchased the company from Dad.

CHAPTER 3

The Glen's Market's Associate

The Key to the Culture: 51 Percent of the Reason
for the Culture, and the Company's Greatest Asset

*The Earth yields its produce and material wealth to support and
enrich mankind through the providence of work relations.*
                                                —John MacArthur

If you worked at Glen's Markets, the E word was never used...NEVER

The word *employee* was outlawed at Glen's somewhere in the late
seventies. Although many companies still call the people who are on
their payroll by the *E* word, that just indicates to me that they do
not get it. Creating an intentional culture is not within the grasp of
understanding for their leadership.

Disney calls their team "Cast Members." After taking ten of our
top leadership team to Orlando for a week to go through Disney's
Cast Member and Leadership Training Programs, one starts to
understand that there is no doubt that a Cast Member understands
what their part is in the process of taking care of the customer. Like
a part in a play, there is a loss if it is not addressed intentionally and
with determination. Likewise, we did everything we could to inten-

tionally offer an atmosphere where our associates felt like they were an integral part of the Glen's Organization.

Some companies have even taken a greater step beyond, like the one who titles their receptionist director of first impressions. Is there any doubt what the first responsibility is for that receptionist? Surely not. He or she, without a doubt, understands and knows the part they play in the company they are a part of.

We wanted our team to feel more worth than just doing a job and getting a paycheck. Their value to the company was so much greater than that; hence, it was important to help them realize it. In fact, it wasn't just "important," it was critical!

Of course, what good is a name change if it is not effective? One key example that sticks in my mind is a day I was walking near the checkout in one of our stores. There was obviously a new cashier at one of the registers. As she turned to the young high school man bagging groceries, she commented about something that I didn't quite hear, nor did I want to ask either one of them with the chance of embarrassing them. But I did hear his reply: "We're not employees around here. At Glen's, we are associates. We are a big part of this company. What we do makes a difference." The cashier wouldn't have met me yet, and the young man didn't see me. I left it that way, but I never forgot it. That's called "intentional culture" at its finest.

A re-generating culture is priceless! Although it needs to continually be fueled and intentionally fed, it can be compared to an automobile from which its own momentum empowers its force and energy to keep moving. Without intentional focus, your culture will still become self-generating, but it will be based on where the weakest link will slowly pull down the next weakest, and that weak link will pull down the next weakest link, and so it will go until the culture will be no culture; however, that in itself will become the new norm for the culture, not a desirable one but one all too often you witness in floundering businesses.

A successful culture is one that re-generates itself in a positive and intentional way. We called our associates our Glen's Family. The mission statement on our associate handbook stated, "We are people working with people, serving people."

We always said, "We were people working with people, serving people," We just happened to be in the grocery business.

We were told by Spartan Stores that Glen's was the first retailer to put together an associate handbook that assisted the associate to better understand what was expected of them and what they could expect. That credit goes to Bill Brown, our personnel director at the time.

The customer comes second...period!

I know this sounds strange and sounds like something that many could say, but to follow through with it and live it is tougher than one might think. That is unless you really believe it. Family *is* family. And at Glen's Markets, we believed it.

However, from our perspective, it only made sense. If our associates were treated right, well trained, and had a feeling of being appreciated, empowered, and of being a valuable part of the team, why wouldn't they treat our customers in the same manner? Happy and productive associates produce happy and satisfied customers. As simple as it is, it only makes sense. Leadership may be "leadership" but who has the most contact with the customer and especially the last contact with the customer as they are leaving the business? The cashier and the person bagging the groceries. Statistics show that the final experience a person has exiting a business will impact them more than most anything else as to whether they return or not. Our front-end associates were priceless in customer relationships.

Communicate, communicate, communicate

When starting to talk about what is most important in building a culture, I absolutely have no idea where to start. I do know that if a guy winks at a pretty girl in the dark, the only one that's going to feel good about it is the guy doing the winking.

About everything we did at Glen's was communicated in our quarterly newsletter, *Off the Shelf.* Hence, as we wander through this story of Glen's, there will be countless pictures taken from our *Off the Shelf* publication.

Even when starting a quarterly newsletter, we invited our associates to get involved, first by offering a little contest for naming it. Carolyn Weislik, our front-end manager in our Charlevoix store came up with the fitting name *Off the Shelf.*

Carolyn Weislik (Front End Mgr. in Charlevoix)
receiving check for naming the *Off the Shelf*, the future
for communications with our Associates

OFF THE SHELF

MARKETS
Glen's
NEWSLETTER

| VOLUME 12 NUMBER 7 | A PUBLICATION OF GLEN'S MARKETS | JULY 1990 |

UP FRONT!

Whew! Company-wide, we sure have had a busy first half of the year. With our major addition in Houghton Lake getting finished, our remodeling in Rose City, our new store opening in Cadillac, the purchase of the B & C Supermarket in Cheboygan, our new store opening in Oscoda (Welcome Oscoda Associates!) and our remodeling that was just finished in Kalkaska... It has put an added burden on many of our areas around the company. A BIG **THANK YOU** *to all who helped in getting these locations opened... Whether you actually drove to a store to help or you chipped in a little more to help cover at your home location, I know I can say on behalf of all of us, that we truly appreciate your efforts.*

As a company, we are having a busy year sales wise too. I know it's not that far behind us that we remember how our 39th anniversary sale really seemed to kick the summer off. For the benefit of knowing where we stand for our "Associate Achievement Bonus Plan", we are having great sales increases, but are running a little behind in our budgets in the area of Gross and Labor Control. My guess is with the great summer we are having, by fall we should be right in line with our budgets for this year. If you are a Department Manager, you know what your controls are... If you do not have the responsibility of a department, you can still do your part through excellent customer service and attacking shrink in everything that you do.

I know summer is half gone, but we do still have the best part left. I challenge you to enjoy it with those that you love to be with... Remember happiness shouldn't be your goal throughout life, it should be your journey.

Thank you for your continued support and commitment,

Glen Catt
President

Personal Profile
GLEN B. CATT
Store Director - Oscoda

"Growing up in Kalkaska, I didn't feel any pressure being Glen Catt's son and C. Glen's grandson. I grew up as me," stated the "younger" Glen of his childhood.

Glen started out his grocery career at the young age of fourteen in Kalkaska where he was a Service Clerk. After attending college in Traverse City, he came back to Glen's as Frozen Food Manager in Kalkaska. He transferred to Boyne as Dairy Manager, and was Grocery Manager at Iron Mountain and Sault Ste. Marie. Glen became Assistant Manager at West Branch and then left for Spartan for a year and worked in their Wings of the Future program. Next he was Assistant Manager at Alpena and then eventually the Store Manager ... and now Store Director at our new, beautiful store in Oscoda.

It was a beautiful Monday morning the day I went to Oscoda to get information for my feature on that store. I had called Glen the week before to set my time of arrival and make sure that I'd picked a good day. He told me, "Just for you, Jackie, I'll set my Department Manager's meeting at 9:00 so you won't have to get up so early to drive here." Ha! When I got there at 8:40 their meeting was just about wrapped up. He got out of it really fast by saying that he was just getting the meeting out of the way to free up his people for me. Since he offered me coffee and a roll right after that... I chose to believe him!

I see a youthful, vibrant personality in Glen to go along with his store experience, and it seems to be a perfect complement to a similar personality in his Operations Manager, Ray Shelley. In both interviews, I sensed the excitement in their spirit, and the excitement in their approach to this new challenge. Yet, in both, I saw a maturity in their dealings with others.

continued on back page . . .

An example of the front page of Off the Shelf.
This article actually featured Glen B. Catt as the newly
named Store Mgr. of the new Oscoda location

Show sincere and honest appreciation

People do not care how much you know until they know how much you care. Let me say that again. *People do not care how much you know until they know how much you care.*

Back to having an associate handbook, what better door can you open for an associate to succeed than, first thing, laying out what the company expects from them and what they can expect from the company.

Obviously, the key in any relationship should start with simply listening to people and giving them your undivided attention—eye contact. We all know people who when we are conversing with them, they are looking around. Are they listening? Or when they are talking to us and they're looking around. Who are they really talking to? Talk then becomes cheap.

A smile is the easiest jester you can make. A sincere "thank you" is the most powerful word that shows appreciation.

Each of our associates wore a name tag. It was mandatory, including for me. This was obvious for our associates to get to know them better and for our customers to be able to identify the associate working with them. Likewise, with the number of associates we had in different locations, it allowed our leadership team to relate in more of a one-to-one relationship. I recently received a comment on Facebook from Jared Armstrong, whose father, Fred, was one of our great store managers. Jared said, "I remember being very young with my father visiting the offices. I was going to spend the day with him at work, but you told me I needed a name tag, so you gave me yours. You would not believe the faces of everyone I encountered that day." Everyone wore a name tag!

Being honest sometimes doesn't include giving the answer someone was hoping for, but it reflects not only appreciation but respect for a person's intelligence. Most people do not wish to be brushed over; they want the truth even if sometimes the truth hurts. However, as one in leadership, there is a tact in sharing the truth without crushing them because of your position. Sometimes, one just has to say, "I'm not sure if I have the right words, but I want to be honest with you." People aren't anymore foolish than you are, although in our egos (as part of leadership), we often think we know pretty much all there is to know. People know when you are full of hot air or sharing honest answers with a sensitivity to their feelings. Probably too often, I would find myself saying, "Did that come across okay?" "Does that make sense?" "Did I answer your question?"

There is not a word that is more important in a person's mind than their name. At the time we sold our grocery operation, our highest point of employment for associates would be during the summer months (due to all our operations being in tourist areas of northern and upper Michigan). With about 2,500 associates, it would have been impossible for me, or any of our team, to remember everyone's names (perhaps one exception was Bill Brown, our director of personnel, but I'll talk about Bill later). More often than I could remember, an associate in one of the stores would say to me, "It always amazes me that you remember my name. That really means a lot to me." To which I would probably reply, in simple honesty, "Thank you (i.e., Sally), and as long as you continue to wear your name tag, and my eyes allow me to read your name out twenty feet, I always will," which I would end in a large smile. Truth is, she knew, and I knew she knew. We would then both chuckle.

At Glen's, as the "founders" son and later president and principal, I realized that the words and the actions that rolled off my tongue carried more weight than I wish they did. On the other hand, there are statements that the CEO can do for the culture that no one else can do. At Glen's, we did appreciate each of our associates, and we knew there were many ways we could show it.

In December, a CHRISTmas card was mailed to each of our associates, which I personally signed. On their birthday, each associate was mailed a birthday card, which I personally signed. On the anniversary date of an associate with Glen's, whether it was one year or their thirty-first year, each associate received a card thanking them for—years with the Glen's Family and thanking them for such, which I personally signed and would often comment on. Any associate who received a promotion received a card or letter congratulating them for the well-deserved promotion and thanking them for their commitment. (And I was aware of others in the office who would also take the time to drop associates a note on their promotion.) Obviously, I signed a lot of cards and letters. Many of them I would fill out a month ahead of time while either flying on a plane somewhere or riding in a car heading to stores with one of the other team members. Sometimes when I got a little behind, I would take them home, but for the benefit of my family, I really tried not to do that though.

Did I have time to do all these? Surely not. Toward the later years of Glen's, we were talking over six thousand cards being sent out a year. Thankfully for me, I had Rosemary Ross, my number one hidden, secret weapon. Rosemary was my executive assistant, one of the most effective right-hand people a CEO could ever have. She would and could do anything! She made me look good. I miss her! Her little four-foot, eleven-inch structure was a giant in the effectiveness of my position as the top leader at Glen's Markets.

CHRISTmas with our associates was an important event for us. Obviously, early on, we could hold one party at a township hall and then later on moved to a larger venue at a local resort with the associates in Kalkaska, Grayling, and East Jordan driving in (maximum of 40-mile drive for anyone). We would always invite an associate's spouse, full-time or part-time, and unmarried adults could bring a friend of the opposite sex. All the high school students were invited also. As more stores were added, we had to break into more parties with three to four stores at an event. For many of us, every weekend in December was going to store parties, often a couple in a row, which, somewhat tiring, was always an awesome experience.

Typical for grocery stores, throughout the year, various vendors and salespeople would give stores "premiums"—gifts for purchasing product or for promoting their product. We had a strict policy that "no one" was allowed to take a premium home. This accomplished three things: first, it helped eliminate any kind of challenge where a vendor received special treatment in exchange for a "gift"; second, it eliminated one or two people in a store, getting all the premiums given at that store; and third, those hundreds of premiums throughout the year were then split up, wrapped (each by our office staff), and given away as door prizes at each of our CHRISTmas parties. Many were really pretty exceptional gifts.

Throughout the year, our personnel department would collect pictures from each of the stores of individuals and groups of associates. The evening of the parties, the pictures for those stores represented would be put on a large screen with the recycling song by Carly Simon, "Nobody Does It Better." In case you may not know or remember the lyrics, it starts off:

> Nobody does it better
> Makes me feel sad for the rest
> Nobody does it half as good as you
> Baby, you're the best

That may sound a little corny, but when, year after year, the same song, and even some of the same pictures (although they would be as current as possible and often funny ones), would find associates yelling, cheering, and applauding for their coworkers, you realize that as corny as this was, there was a great camaraderie building. A ten- to twelve-minute piece of entertainment became a key culture-building element each year. When Denny Freeman first proposed it, I too thought it was a little goofy, but the proof was in the pudding. Denny was awesome when it came to understanding people and personally touching their lives. It was what he did best.

A typical CHRISTmas Party at Glen's

Leadership would dress up as elves to hand out
gifts (Fred Armstrong on right, started in H.S. in
Kalkaska and became Grayling store manager)

*If associates are treated right and well trained, they
will feel empowered, valuable, and appreciated*

Why would a company hire people and not train them? Yet we see it all the time in the business we frequent but often don't desire to return to. I remember a time when I was an assistant manager. It was July 2 (the third of July was always the busiest day of the year for our stores, and the day before wasn't too far behind). A new cashier was hired in the store I was at, and she continued to fumble throughout the day. I still remember her name was Yvonne. She was so frustrated later in the day. I asked her if she was okay (the store being so busy, I was spending most of the day bagging groceries). She said she had never done this before, but because the individual who hired her was busy, he said, "Just get behind the register. It's pretty basic. After a little while, you will figure it out." It's unfortunate for Yvonne. I think she may have been able to become a good associate. It wasn't too many months later when I was then the store manager. I had to ask her to leave. I believe even a mediocre individual (in their mind, self-confidence, and abilities) can excel if they are trained and given the attention that they need.

The basics for developing a good associate are obviously the following:

- Train them, coach them, and then "inspect what you expect."
- Catch them doing something good, compliment them, and encourage them for it.
- Always give praise verbally or in writing (in front of others is always a plus).
- Never give even the slightest negative direction or reprimand in front of others, and never put it in an email, text, or writing. Of course, if the associate has been addressed about the same issue before, well, then it needs to be documented, but privately with them.

The need to have an effective but more so consistent discipline system is extremely important. It addresses the need for consistency, it reflects that you do inspect what you expect, it addresses problem associates and associates that just flat screw up, it creates a standard from which associates know what is expected within the culture of the organization, and it creates a standard, and if managed, it also protects the organization from the abusive side of the labor laws. A program too stringent, and associates do not feel the opportunity to be themselves, be creative, add their "own" personality and talents to the organization. A program too lax creates sloppiness and lends to loopholes where one rotten apple can affect the whole bunch.

When addressing an associate, we tried to be sure to distinguish between personal performance and personal attitude. All too often, when an associate is being corrected in their actions, second-guessing ends up prevailing. The self-consciousness of the human race has a tendency to take things personal. If a leader is addressing the job performance of an individual, that needs to be clarified so that there is not any misunderstanding. Likewise, if the correction needs to be in the area of attitude, then that too needs to be clarified. Whether addressing performance or attitude, it is still most effective to end the conversation with a positive comment. I have had many individuals whom, while addressing a performance issue, I've been able to then tell them how much I always appreciate their positive attitude with fellow associates and customers alike and vice versa.

Intentional leadership understands the difference in knowing that you can compliment the positive and then focus on addressing the challenges. But as I already mentioned, it is good to always leave the conversation with a positive note; this allows the associate to be assured you desire for them to stay and that you have confidence in their being a great asset with the company.

For us, we found it is much easier to address performance than attitude. However, if you desire a positive, self-encouraging culture (both for your associates and for your customers), addressing less-than-desired attitudes is extremely important. If I were to guess, I would say that we asked more individuals to seek employment somewhere else more often over attitude than we did over performance. Either way, our program laid out below was extremely effective in helping good associates to make a positive adjustment and yet eliminate those who chose not to (when followed).

The Glen's Market Associate Discipline Program was actually quite simple:

- The first time an associate "messed up," there was a verbal addressing. This would be done on a one-on-one basis, and in most cases, this would eliminate any need for future addressing—often because it was just a onetime thing with the associate, or the associate just didn't realize that they had done wrong. And again, this was never to happen in front of another associate or customer.
- In the event that the associate repeated the same action within a month, there would be a verbal addressing, normally with the associate's immediate supervisor or someone else in a leadership position as a witness. The discussion would be documented, and it would be placed in their file. If the first verbal addressing hadn't rerouted the associate's actions, most often this addressing would.

- In the event that the associate repeated the same action within a window of time which was rare, but of course happened at times, the associate would be offered a day off *with* pay to decide if they wanted to continue working at Glen's. Likewise, during that time, the store management would consider if they desired to have the associate continue with their employment at Glen's. When the associate returned to work, both parties would discuss the future of the associate with Glen's Markets. Most times when the associate returned, they became a great associate, but there were also times when the associate returned and management decided that the associate's employment was not going to be continued.

Through this program, many weak associates became strong associates. The program also allowed a firm but fair system for eliminating an associate's employment. Only in situations like dishonesty (dishonestly was not tolerated, period!) was an associate terminated on the spot. The program, if consistent, allowed other associates to know undesirable situations would be addressed. And through this program, if consistent, it allowed the company to avoid being sued for unfair employment practices that would otherwise lead to abusive unemployment payments. Although a firm but fair discipline program may not be considered a culture maker/breaker, it surely was. Associates were given the opportunity to understand what was expected and make personal adjustments, which would result in benefiting them and benefiting the company. The challenge, as it always is, is to strive to treat everyone equally, no matter their years with the company or their position in the company.

Of course, dishonesty was totally not to be tolerated—dishonesty being lying, cheating, or stealing. Well, one might say that goes without discussion, but does it always?

One of our most effective store managers, actually managing our largest facility, personally cashed and pocketed a couple of vendor refund checks, not a large amount compared to what a store manager could scheme, perhaps less than $300.00. Nevertheless, when another associate in the store reported his suspicions, we asked the manager and his wife to come to the general offices to discuss it. As always, there was more going on than expected; however, we were convinced not in a dishonest way. Through our conversation, it was discovered that our man had an alcohol problem. He agreed to go through a recovery program, which, at Glen's Markets, we covered the expense. He was temporarily suspended, but it was with his pay and benefits. As suspected, over the next six weeks while he was in rehab, the feedback coming back from stores was most interesting. We heard secondhand comments like the following: "Being one of the number one store managers, they will never terminate him for just three hundred bucks." "The company policy has no leniency for dishonesty." "I'll bet Glen and Denny will not break C. Glen's policy for anyone. Dishonesty is dishonesty." Although Denny Freeman and I talked a little about what would happen when our friend got out of rehab, we talked very little and definitely did not share our conversations.

Upon the individual returning to the offices with his wife, they shared how extremely appreciative they were for the continued employment and support through the alcohol recovery program. However, when we announced to them that we had no option but to terminate their employment with the company because of dishonesty, they became very livid, upset, and left abruptly. The good news is over the years, we have heard that this individual has stayed dry. The effect on the culture at Glen's Markets? Over the next few months visiting stores, numerous, countless associates would bring up their support and respect for the stance we took with an associate that we valued and loved. I suspect the impact that our interest for the well-being of our associates and the perils of dishonesty were ingrained a little deeper into our culture.

We believed in helping to create an atmosphere that offered self-motivation, a desire to improve, and an enhanced self-confidence. We felt strong that enhanced self-confidence would equal a winner in anyone's books, certainly for the benefit of other associates, for our customers, and again for our organization. We believed it, we encouraged it, and we benefited from it.

Zig Ziglar said, "You can get everything in life you want if you help enough other people get what they want." I believe everyone has a desire to "do better" whatever that may be in their mind. Along with position training, departmental training, and various leadership training programs, at Glen's Markets, we also offered the Zig Ziglar *Born to Win* seminars. If you are not aware of the Zig Ziglar programs, it would be worth your effort to seek to get a better understanding of it.

We offered a four-day (one day a week over four weeks) course using the Zig Ziglar *Born to Win* and *See You at the Top* books. These were full 8:00 a.m. to 4:30 p.m. days that involved workbooks and individual involvement covering sixteen sessions during the four weeks. Of course, the company covered 100 percent of the cost of the material, while each associate would be responsible for their own time (store managers would schedule accordingly) and for their own travel to the seminars.

One of the books used during our •Born to Win• classes

Born to Win book

With over two thousand associates eventually going through the Zig program, it also allowed us to intimately get to know many of our family even better. Denny Freeman, who originally suggested offering the course to our associates, started teaching the first couple of years. As it grew, George Brown and Kevin Hanson, both also part of our human resource team, took the lead. The kickoff session would always involve myself and Denny present (with each of us obviously sharing our 2 cents), and like all meetings at Glen's, it would be kicked off with everyone standing and doing a group cheer. Of course, graduation was always a big deal with the store managers and district managers from the associate's stores also present (sometimes fellow associates of those graduating would also attend on their own time). Graduation was always open to all, obviously with a lot of cheering and most often tears of new found self-worth and expanded perceptions. The great thing about the human mind is once it is expanded, it never returns to its original shape.

Denny Freeman (left) and Bert Taylor (right) leading a cheer at the beginning of a meeting... we always started with a cheer!

Born to Win graduating class

Born to Win graduating class

Even Dad graduated from •Born to Win•

Again, associates took this course on their own time. Each store manager would work around their schedule so that they could be off that day. Likewise, for those driving from other stores to the seminar location, their travel expenses would be their own. I always remember my dad saying, if you give someone something for free, they won't appreciate it as much if they have to work for it a little. Obviously, if associates were going to be paid for these seminars, everyone would have taken it, but would they have absorbed as much if they didn't "have a skin in the game"? I don't think so. Glen's Markets paid for all the books and all the workbooks and supplied beverages and lunch during the day. Upon graduation, each associate who had attended all the sessions would also receive a certificate for a paid day off to be coordinated with their store management team. This day could be at their discretion, but it would need to be coordinated at least a week in advance so that their store manager or department manager could arrange the schedule accordingly.

The Dallas-based Zig Ziglar organization told us that Glen's Markets had become the number one purchaser of their books and materials. Zig, himself, called our offices to speak to my father, who was still the president of our company. He was extremely impressed when our receptionist, Karen Gregor, answered the phone and said, "It's a great day at Glen's Markets, how may I help you?" It was a "Zig"-proclaimed version of how you should be answering the phone.

The success of the Zig Ziglar program was instant; hence, we continued it. It was successful even to the point that we had some associates say the following: "I always wanted to pursue this (career)," or "Do something different with my life," or "Go back to school," or "Move to (wherever)." "The Ziglar program has built my confidence, and now I'm going to leave Glen's and pursue my dream." We heard that more than once, but although we hated to lose them, if we couldn't get excited for that individual too, well, I guess our heart and best interest for them wasn't as true as it should have been in the first place.

Word of the Zig Ziglar program got around to where the Gaylord Community School system requested that Denny put the program on for their teachers. Over time, ninety teachers graduated from the program. Likewise, the northern Michigan departments of social workers also requested. Over a number of Saturdays, 280 social workers were exposed to and graduated from the Glen's Market's Zig Ziglar program also.

One of the items that Denny added to the program, in the beginning, was that he would ask those present to randomly throw out attributes that they felt a leader would need to have. After writing down twenty-five to thirty adjectives on a flip chart (and taping them to the wall) that would describe what people thought a leader should have, he would then go over them one by one and ask, "Is this a *skilled trait*, or is this an *attitude*?" Those involved would quickly realize that although there are many skills needed to be a leader, the majority of the attributes needed to become a leader are formed by their attitude. I too think this was a key ritual that helped form the Glen's Market Culture. There is nothing like a "new pair of glasses" (a new attitude) to help people see a clearer picture. It goes without being said, prior to the Zig Ziglar program being offered to our hourly associates, all of our salaried leadership went through the program. That attitude and new insight that came from these programs were termed *being Ziglified!*

Realize the resources you have hidden in your team

We would often bring associates together in a store to pick their brain about the operation. If it were to do with something in the front-end operation, who better could give input and insight than cashiers and high school baggers? Looking at changing something in the meat departments, whose input could offer to be extremely valuable than those whom it affected? Did these individuals make the final decisions? Depending on the issue, maybe yes, maybe no. Obviously, top leadership is always accountable, but only a fool wouldn't seek, bringing in the hand-on team for their input.

We also would have annual company improvement committees. These individuals would be pulled from different stores, given a general agenda, but also asked to give input on anything that they found common between their stores that they felt should be considered to be reevaluated or changed. We would always have someone from the top leadership as part of these committees to be the facilitator, make sure no one individual hogged the conversation, and help the discussion along so that an individual wouldn't try to focus a conversation on something that was unique in the store location that they were from.

Needless to say, it was always eye opening and amazing the suggestions that would come from these committees.

Company Improvement Committee Meeting Representatives: (L-R) Kurt Kitchen, Houghton Lake; Judy Mann, Charlevoix; Nancy Funck, Grayling; Susanne Adams, Mancelona; Larry Johnson, Kalkaska; Sally Muzik, West Branch; Julie Barber, Rose City; Debbie Yoder, Mio; Bill Niswander, East Jordan; Leslie Keipert, Roscommon; and Dave Duffield, Gaylord.

One of our annual Company Improvement Committees

Get to know your people and their interests

This doesn't mean just those in leadership but also on the front line where contact with the customer is. To do this, you have to listen and ask questions. Please let me repeat that, listen *and then* ask questions. We learned a lot from each of our associates. "What do you think?" has a powerful impact when you listen. I think many leaders are afraid to ask the opinion of others.

- *What if I don't agree with their answer?* Ask them if it is okay to agree to disagree.
- *I'm the leader. Shouldn't I come up with the answers?* A strong confidence means the best answer is best for the majority, no matter whom it came from.

- *Being the leader, I would probably know better what is needed.* You may be the leader, but how long since you walked in their shoes, since you performed the job they are doing?
- I'm sure you get the picture here.

It is amazing what one can learn when they are not afraid of asking questions and more so not afraid of what they might hear. The goal is to get the best decisions made for the company, for the associates involved, and for the customers. Plus, as already been shared, *Those who help plan the trip, enjoy the ride the most.*

It is also surprising how many times you may find out that an associate had gone to school for something but now is working as a cashier or stocker because they couldn't get into their profession.

We wandered into VHS movies and later DVD movies to rent in our stores, kind of in a minor way (this was something I saw in other stores around the country during my travels). With the growing interest by customers to want to rent a movie (at the time, there weren't the larger movie rental stores like Blockbuster, etc., in our areas), we decided to go rogue and fill a few vacancies in our little shopping centers by opening video rental stores. Dad always said, "If you want a successful business, find a need and want that wasn't being offered and fill it, but fill it in the right way."

Hearing of one of our associates who had pursued a marketing degree but was cashiering for us now, we pulled her out of her checkout line and offered her to head our video rentals. We gave her guidelines and worked closely with her for a short time, and before you know it, we had a small chain of video stores, creating a lot of cash flow. Honestly, the figures didn't look too good on the profit and loss statement, but they offered tremendous depreciation expenses, which we could use as an accounting expense against the total company sales, generating a spin-off of cash flow that helped the rest of the organization. After a number of years, when the market started getting saturated, we sold the stores to a video chain, but we were able to keep them as a tenant in our centers. As for the associate, she became more valuable and was moved into another position in our general offices.

It wasn't uncommon to talk about a position that needed filling, and then someone would share, "You know (such and such) has this talent (or went to school for this). It would be the right fit for his/her interest." We could only get this directly from our store associates.

I remember talking to a young, high school lad working in the meat department of our Grayling store one day. He mainly cleaned up the department after school (we always power washed our meat departments with disinfectant at the end of the day). He was a sharp, high-energy "kid." I asked him what he thought he wanted to do with his life. His reply shocked me. He said, "Someday, I want to have Bert Taylor's job!" Bert was the director of meat operations over all of our meat departments. Well, that young kid, John Rolfe, after high school became a meat cutter and then later became the meat manager in that store. Later, he was promoted to an assistant store manager's position in another store and then moved to become the store manager at another location. And when Bert Taylor retired, John had proven and prepared himself to the point where there was no question who the right person was for the new director of our meat division.

As important as it is to prepare individuals to become promotable, it is likewise (if not more so) important to make those hard decisions to suggest some individuals to seek other employment. Aside from dishonesty or poor performance, a poor attitude or different management/leadership philosophy can be equally detrimental to the intentional culture of a company. Although it's tough to ask someone to vacate your company, sometimes giving them the opportunity to stay on the payroll for two to four weeks to assist them in finding another job can be a well-decided investment.

Of course, one of the toughest challenges is when someone in leadership has developed a close friendship with the associate that needs to leave for culture purposes. We all want to try and make it work, but a decision and a change have to be made. Do you make a decision based on friendship or what is best for the company? Trust me, the culture is always watching.

I remember the first time I faced this. It involved a key associate that I not only was close to but was perhaps my closest friend at the time. In fact, he and his wife and Jeanne and I were almost insepa-rable on the weekends. We had talked a lot about the unrest in the store in which he was the store manager, so we arranged to have him transfer to another location to allow him a fresh start. I was aware that this decision was probably made because of our friendship, but he was a good man but just had an uncanny awkwardness with those who had to answer to him. However, after the move to a different store, that store started having the same challenges. I really didn't know what to do. I told him we may need to make a change, but I knew inside that I wasn't sure I could do that. I literally loved this guy! As it was, "father knows best." My dad saw the picture, stepped in, brought the three of us together, and made the hard decision that I couldn't bring myself to make. It was the right decision, and it had to be made, but relationships fogged up my mind. As it was, to this day (it took a number of years), we are still friends, and as history allows one to look in the crystal ball, I really believe his future career and lifestyle have enhanced because he was forced to move on.

Sometimes for the betterment of the overall operation, you need to hire outside the company

In building and supporting the culture, like everything, there is a balance. Glen's Markets was huge in promoting from within. At one time, twelve out of seventeen of our store managers started out as high school baggers. At the store level, we had never brought someone into a store, from outside the company, for any of the top three or four positions in the store. Although there were a few times we might bring someone in who hadn't had "grocery" experience, put them through a yearlong training program and then promote them, but even then, never to a store manager's position. Culture was too important to trust someone from outside the company to be a quarterback in one of the stores. There actually were twice that my dad had brought individuals into the company and made them store managers. Neither situation worked out, and in both cases, it wasn't that they weren't qualified; it was because they brought their own backpack of culture thinking (or perhaps lack of culture thinking) to the table.

We did realize that sometimes, there may be an element of the business that we just couldn't bring to the standards that we may witness (and envy in a good way) in other similar organizations, but we didn't have the talent within our company to pull from. We only found this out after sticking to the theory of "promoting from within." Nevertheless, the first time, it was a tough decision to go outside the company to seek an individual to be our director of produce. We knew our best produce department wasn't up to what we were seeing in supermarkets around the country, and we just didn't have the talent at the time and, more so, the understanding. Likewise, when we grew to the point of needing someone to oversee our deli departments and our bakery departments, we felt we had to look elsewhere. We were extremely fussy, and it almost always paid off. Although there are times when you need to bring the expertise into your organization, it had better be good because people are watching. If it doesn't work out, it can crush a part of the culture; if it does work out, well, everyone benefits. We found that by working with "head-hunters," they would quite often seek out a specialist, who was working in a large supermarket chain, to suggest an opportunity where they could go from being a "small fish in a large pond to a large fish in a small pond." Our challenge in the interview process was to make sure that their philosophy and attitude for people fit into our culture of associates. One of those few times we searched the industry for talent, we obtained Brian Whitman. Brian was in the marketing department in the offices of Harris Teeter, a chain on the East Coast that at the time had about 180 stores in their chain. Brian left a key position in their marketing to join us in overseeing all of our marketing, shortly afterward becoming our vice president of marketing and merchandising. I believe people like Brian, and Pat Hilley (who had joined us as our director of deli) brought expertise that supported the culture that we needed and wanted, which resulted in taking us to a new level of being the best we could be.

Stan Dizki (left) joined us from Dillon's Supermakets in Colorado as Director of Grocery and Brian Wittman (right) joined us from Harris Teeter in North Carolina (Brian was V.P. of Marketing at the time we sold our stores)

Speaking of great associates, you need to start with the best people you can hire

The first few years of Glen's Markets, the store managers hired the associates for their own store. I was a store manager in Kalkaska in 1969 when my dad announced that an individual named Bill Brown was going to be our personnel director and was going to be hiring all the hourly associates for our (then) six stores. I have to be honest, between us store managers, none of us were too keen on the idea, although it was a time-consuming effort to read applications, interview, and hire individuals. We each enjoyed setting up our own team; thus, this new idea of having someone else hire "our people" was not received well. Each of us knew Bill, but what we knew of him was that my father had hired him from General Motors (downstate) to manage the bowling lanes that he had built. We all knew that he had been doing a wonderful job at Vacationland Lanes, but what would he know about hiring individuals for a grocery store?

The bowling lanes had never been profitable, but Dad said the best benefit he ever got from having that establishment was obtaining Bill Brown. What Bill lacked in grocery experience, he proved invaluable understanding people. Bill developed a standard of what he felt a Glen's Market associate should be, and he did not deviate from that standard. Bill knew that the right attitude and a foundation of interest in doing a good job, along with our training and culture, could produce outstanding associates. Bill ended up working with Denny Freeman (my partner, who, with my sister, purchased the company from Dad), and as we grew, they handpicked individuals like Chris Robinson, George Brown, and Kevin Hansen to work with them in staffing our twenty-six stores. At the time we sold our retail stores, our summer employment was reaching a total of 2,500 associates, a team I continue to be proud to brag about!

We are all aware of some retail chains who have the reputation for hiring any warm body off the street. Now, I totally understand that everyone needs a job, and it is not my intent to discriminate, but if you do not have the culture, the training, and the standards, one needs to be more selective in who they hire. After all, they represent your business to your customer.

An outstanding example of a Glen's Market associate

Early in this book, along with dedicating it to my father, C. Glen Catt, from which, no doubt, the Glen's Market history would never have been started, I also shared the dedication to Norberta Woloszyk. "Bert," as she referred to herself as, was a very special person. She epitomized the living, enthusiastic culture at Glen's Market. Being a middle-aged single woman, she was open to do what she enjoyed, and she did. You know, every business, organization, or branch has one of those. If encouraged, empowered, and appreciated, they shine with such a beacon of light that they become contagious to all those around them. That was Bert Woloszyk.

Bert was the general merchandise manager in our Roger City, Michigan, location. As a resident of the small, potato farming town of nearby Posen, she was also a shining example of the Polish-Catholic heritage that made up over 50 percent of the local population. Bert was stout in structure, probably all those potatoes, but she was full of energy, and spit and vinegar if needed to be. For our key marketing events, and especially the various holidays, Bert was most always the instigator in the decorating of the total store, not just her department but she would recruit everyone to get involved, oftentimes after hours if they couldn't accomplish what they wanted to do and get their responsibilities done in their normally scheduled hours. She was definitely the store's firecracker.

She must have had a closet full of costumes. As for CHRISTmas, she would dress up like either Mrs. Claus or like an elf. For Easter, she would be dressed up like the Easter bunny. For Thanksgiving, she would look like a pilgrim woman who just walked away from serving the Indians. For Halloween, well, who knew what Bert would be dressed as?

But the kicker was she wouldn't just dress up when at the store. On her days off, she would travel to our offices, 65 miles away, and to other Glen's Markets around the north and share her greetings with them. I actually came to find out later that our Roger City store manager would actually allow her to travel around the north, even on days she was on the time clock. (I'm glad we allowed our store managers to focus on the results we wanted and not the politics of business.) He told me that she worked a lot off the clock, she enjoyed what she was doing, and she spread a lot of cheer along the way. It goes without being said that she would be visiting the schools, hospitals, and nursing homes too. Obviously, it was good PR for the store, but then again, the Glen's was the main supermarket in Rogers City. Hence, things like this are the reason why.

In the middle of a Spartan Stores board meeting in Grand Rapids, Michigan, over 250 miles from Roger City, the week prior to Easter, there was a knock on the boardroom door. The corporate

CFO (chief financial officer) was the closest to the door, so he got up to answer the knock. There was Bert, dressed up like the Easter bunny with goodies for everyone in the room. Although it resulted in a very good and fun experience, initially, it caught me off guard as I was sitting across the table from the door; hence, after Bert left, I gave a little apology and more explanation. To my surprise, the comments were more about the great culture we had at Glen's rather than anyone concerned about having the board meeting interrupted. As it was, Bert made many other visits to the Spartan Stores offices, becoming a welcomed friend of Pat Quinn, Spartan's president.

Bert may have been a little outside the realm of our typical Glen's associates, but other than her extra, outside-the-store activities, we had been blessed by a large number of "Berts" in our culture. Although she was special, she wasn't alone.

Norberta was also the only associate who we had ever lost due to an accident within the stores. Unfortunately, as she was going beyond what was expected, decorating for a fall promotion, she was on top of one of the upright freezer cases when she tripped and fell, striking her head on the floor, never to recover consciousness. I am sure her send-off to meet her Creator was probably the largest funeral that little Posen, Michigan, had ever experienced. Our loss was His gain. I am also sure she has continued to decorate heaven with her bubbly, positive, contagious personality.

Norberta "Bert" Woloszyk, May 9, 1943–September 18, 1994

Myself with Bert…one very, very special person.

L-R Jackie Bordo (H.R. Dept), Bert in Easter
bunny costume, and Bill Brown

CHAPTER 4

At Glen's Markets, We Celebrated Everything

Successful and unsuccessful people do not vary greatly in their abilities. They vary in their desires to reach their potential.

—John Maxwell

At Glen's Markets, we put our associates first. We knew our associates were the greatest element to our success. We understood that every associate, no matter what position they were performing in our company, played a vital part in the intentional operation of our organization. We realized that each associate was a creation of God, no different than each of us; they may or may not have a family to provide for, but they had their own personal interests, desires, goals, and wish lists. We also understood that in most cases, each of our associates would spend more time awake at their position at Glen's Markets, then they probably would with their family and/or friends. Hence, it was important to us, extremely important to us that we create an atmosphere where being an associate at Glen's Markets was not just a job but as much of a rewarding part of their life that we could make it. Other than the Friday paycheck, which in reality isn't a benefit but an expected, it was the greatest way we could show our appreciation and the value that they had to the overall family of Glen's.

We celebrated everything.

CHRISTtmas dinners

I have already touched on an early tradition that Dad started as CHRISTmas dinners for all of our associates (I write CHRISTmas a little differently because I wish to not ever leave Christ out of CHRISTmas). But they were a special time of the year and an opportunity for different stores to gather together. With the number of promotions people received, which included moving to another location, and the times that associates may drive to another store to assist in an event or the camaraderie created in team events (to be mentioned later), many associates became friends with others working in stores close by. It always warmed my heart at one of the dinners when I would hear one spouse say to another spouse, "Hey, I want you to meet a friend of mine that works in the (adjoining) store."

Special event parties

Now, we weren't a party company, but we did have our share of get togethers, like the following:

- At a key anniversary for the company, that is, twenty-five years, thirty years, etc. On the thirtieth anniversary of Glen's (because we started in the 50's), we held a company-wide fifties party.

Picture from Glen's 50's party

Picture from Glen's 50's party

Picture from one of Glen's bowling parties

•Off the Shelf• pictures from one of Glen's annual golf events

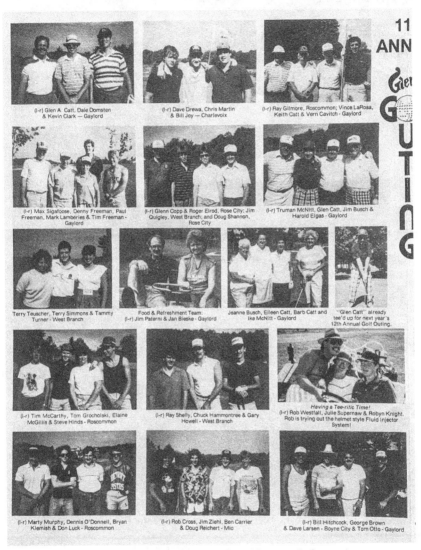

Pictures from •Off the Shelf• golf event (left page)

Pictures from •Off the Shelf• golf event (right page)

- I cannot overstate the celebrations we would have for those graduating from the Zig Ziglar seminars; hence, I'll mention it again.

- New store openings, we would get the new and promoted associates from that store together and celebrate the new store, new addition, or whatever. In our advertising (covering all the stores, as a way to continue to pull everyone together as one family, including our customers), we would include the local store leadership in the advertising. Obviously, this would send a message to all associates and to our customers that we were proud of our team. It was also a small way to allow such associates to become local celebrities for the week in their community and help them to become introduced.

Tim Freeman,
Alpena South Store Director States

Using Associates in our adv's

JAN BIESKE, OUR CHEYBOYGAN STORE DIRECTOR, IS DISPLAYING A SWEET TREAT YOU COULD ENJOY!

Using Associates in our adv's

Using Associates in our adv's (Skip Gilbert, Kalkaska Store Mgr.)

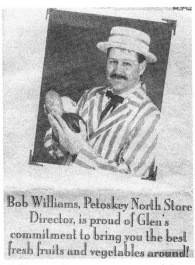

Using Associates in our adv's

Denny in our adv

We guarantee it! You can count on it!

Ken Helsel, Store Director   Glen A. Catt, President

Part of our opening adv for Cadillac with
Store Mgr. Ken Helsel and myself

- Obviously, Halloween and special marketing events couldn't go without allowing (and encouraging) associates to dress up. Again, this was an early tradition that my father started.

Montage of Halloween pics

Ring Master Glen Catt

Pictures from Halloween dress-up (Even
Dad got involved in the early years)

In the office were Betty Dinkel, Keith
Catt and Shari Catt.

Pictures from Halloween dress-up

Gaylord Manager Del Lewis

Pictures from Halloween dress-up

Dave Duffield, Frank Fallon. Cathy Jenkinson, Ruth House, Linda Hayes, Dianne Engel.

Pictures from Halloween dress-up

Dan Hlywa, Mike Grocock, Jim Brandt, Richard Beals, Ray Gilmore.

Pictures from Halloween dress-up

Pictures from Halloween dress-up

Pictures from Halloween dress-up

Pictures from Halloween dress-up (a dept theme)

Another Halloween dress-up (l-R George Brown—
Human Resource Director, Cheryl Kester-Jankoviak—
one of. the exceptional Associates in Cheboygan,
Kevin Clark - Director of General Merchandise, and
Chris Robinson - Human Resource Specialist

- Often times, high school kids are used and abused in a business, but we realized their value, realizing that one day their families were going to be a customer of Glen's Markets, and we also hoped that a good share of them would consider making a career in the grocery business also.

  Hence, each year, we celebrated our high school seniors with a special banquet of appreciation, and we highlighted them in our quarterly *Off the Shelf* publication.

  Likewise, Western Michigan University offered one of the few food distribution courses in the country, so we offered a few WMU Scholarships each year to those showing interest in attending the program.

Graduating H.S. Seniors in •Off the Shelf•

One of the annual H.S. Senior Banquets

Announcement our annual WMU Scholarships

- Obviously, we gave service awards to our associates for five years, ten years, fifteen years, twenty years, and every continuing five years.

  Early on, we would hold a banquet each year, but later we incorporated this into our Annual Stakeholders Meeting (explained later).

Off the Shelf pic of associates receiving service pins

Although Associates received their pins on their
anniversary with our company, here is one of the
annual •off the Shelf• highlighting service awards

5 YEAR SERVICE AWARDS

Spencer Payne, Todd Buck, Tom Grocholski, Sault Ste. Marie

Roy Prough, Greg Hanes, Ed Scholl, Sault Ste. Marie

Teresa Skrobecki, Connie Miller, Karen Sawfford, Mancelona

Back Row: Kevin Clark, Gaylord; Jason Orban, Harold LeMont, Danny Lewis and Ken Nefske. Front Row: Mark Wood, Glen Catt, Ken Bade, Ceil Dembny, Rose Brandon and Bert Woloszyk, from our Alpena and Rogers City Stores

Ray Shelley, Dawn Lutz, Jeff Fisher and Denise Hisscock, West Branch

Leslie Wright, Bob Woolcox, Yvonne Frazho and Dianna Hiser, Mio

Barb Burks, East Jordan

Gregg Bragg, Lynn Kavalunas, Kelly Kingen, Maryjo Marciniak, West Branch

Gayle Black, Connie Morton, Nancy Sawicki, Sandy Lackenbucher, Gaylord

Jackie Burdo, Lon Hansen, Terie Kidder, Bonnie Huff, Gaylord

Sandy Scott; presenter Bill Noeske, Store Mgr.; Roger Elrod and Lynn Barber; Rose City

Chuck Burnett, Kim Norman, Deb Wallington, Tanya Gretzinger, Tom Sawicki, Store Mgr. (presenter); Houghton Lake

Mark Lamberies and Mike Holcomb, Gaylord

Marty Murphy, Barb Fletemier, Karen Willoughby, Gail VanNuck, Sue Ritter, Ken LaPrad; Grayling

Carlajean Gingerich, Dan Kucharek, Mike Mead, Robyn Jorgenson, Heidi Mead; Grayling

Jean Weber, Dave Rusself, Vern Vogelheim, Mike Shank, Roy Kitson, Roxanne Sippel, Vic Urman, Boyne City

Tim Brown, Pat Bresnahan, Mary Pifer, Dawn Reid, Ken Sitkiewicz; Gaylord

Laura Eaton, Diane Grice, Deb Hammontree, Karen Herrmann; Boyne City

Bonnie Edwards, Gail Burkhart, Robin Hill, Barb Carroll, Jackie Syzmanski, Sylvia Francisco; Lewiston

Steve Leazier, Dave Peck, Judy Donnelly, Kitty Chase, Steve Gauthier, Tracy Donaldson, Cheryl Bauman; Charlevoix

—8—

Sevice awards in •Off the Shelf•

- We celebrated promotions. We really celebrated promotions. We wanted associates to see that a job well done did not go without notice. Most often when an individual would receive a promotion that included moving to another store (was never a mandatory move), that would obviously open their old position for someone to be promoted, which often would then open another position for someone.

  As I mentioned, I would send a letter to everyone receiving a promotion. But we would also list everyone who received a promotion in our quarterly *Off the Shelf* publication. Everyone loves to see their name in print, especially since we mailed the publications to our associate's homes; thus, their family could also be brought into what the company was doing.

- Obviously, we celebrated outstanding performance. Each quarter, we would hold an Outstanding (i.e., Dairy Manager) of the District. We had different store districts that would consist of six to eight stores in a district (each district had a district manager who would work with each store manager and team and liaison between the stores and the general offices). Each quarter, an individual from each district would be named "Outstanding" in their department (decided on by the district manager, store manager, and divisional directors [i.e., director of grocery, director of meats, director of produce, etc.]). The awarded department managers would receive a plaque, and they would be highlighted in our quarterly *Off the Shelf* publication. Of course, they would receive a letter or a card from me.

  Then at the end of the year, those awarded each quarter would qualify for the "Outstanding" (department manager) for the year for that district. That announcement and award would also be presented at our Annual Stakeholders Meeting.

Pics of associates receiving Outstanding Awards

Associates receiving individual Outstanding
Awards at our Annual Stakeholder's Meeting

Associates receiving individual Outstanding
Awards at our Annual Stakeholder's Meeting

Associates receiving individual Outstanding
Awards at our Annual Stakeholder's Meeting

Associates receiving individual Outstanding
Awards at our Annual Stakeholder's Meeting

Pic of store teams receiving Outstanding Awards

Store Leadership Team receiving Outstanding Team in their District Award in their district at our Annual Stakeholder's Meeting (Glen B. Catt, bottom left, was their District Mgr.)

Store Leadership Team receiving Outstanding Team in their District Award in their district at our Annual Stakeholder's Meeting (John Nemeth, top left, was their District Mgr.

- So what was our Annual Stakeholders Meeting?

A stakeholder is anyone who has a stake in the operation and performance of the Company. At Glen's Markets, our annual stakeholder's get-togather, the key individuals whom we purchased products from were invited... like the President of Spartan Stores, and many of the VP's whom we worked with. The bank officials whom we worked with were invited. There were key vendors that worked with our associates that were invited. In total, perhaps a couple of dozen key individuals outside the Glen's Organization, but it was important for us to have them witness our company celebrating our Glen's Family.

And obviously our associates were invited, along with their spouse or significant others. Needless to say, we were pretty limited on locations in northern Michigan that could host a party that large. Although it was our desire that all could attend, we know that isn't always possible; however, we would celebrate the evening with 1,500–1,800 stakeholders in attendance.

What evening could be complete without food and entertainment (sometimes pretty corny by our top leadership). And we would celebrate people. The Outstanding Associates of the Year for each department from each district, would be announced. The WMU Scholarship winners would be introduced. Associates who had celebrated key anniversaries with the family would be introduced. The energy during the evening would be extremely high from the crowd as different associates from their store were brought to the stage and introduced for their accomplishments. And all this would obviously be recorded by camera to be included in our next *Off the Shelf* publication.

This get-together would allow both Denny and myself to share personal words of appreciation and encouragement for our associates. *And* again, having the various executives from banks and wholesale companies that we worked with would make a statement in itself to them.

Group picture from one of our Annual Stakeholder's Meetings

Group picture from one of our Annual Stakeholder's
Meetings (you always gotta have food...)

Part of our Leadership team entertaining at one of our Annual Stakeholder's Meeting. A little Wizard of Oz, •There's no place like Glen's, There's no people like Glen's people!•

- Spartan Stores, our main wholesaler source, used to have annual conventions. We would normally, with no doubt, have the largest group of attendees as we would invite all of our store managers and our office leadership with their spouses. When Spartan started cutting back on their annual event, we created the Glen's Market's Leadership Retreat.

   We would hold these annually at a northern Michigan resort and, again, invite each of our store managers, office leadership, and their spouses. This would be a four-day, three-night event with little business. Mornings would include brief entertainment and a speaker focused on personal/relationship development but no business, other than some monkey business. The afternoons would have activities like golf, fishing, sailing, etc., available. And the evenings would involve dinner (most often a theme, outdoor event) and some light entertainment.

   The intent of this retreat would be, again, to show our appreciation to our top team and their spouses, offer some personal growth insight, just let our hair down, and of course build on relationships.

Myself and one of our
entertainers at one of our
Annual Leadership retreats at
a Northern Michigan resort

Vern Cavitch, Director of
Advertising, letting go of his pride
and helping to entertain our top
leadership team. (Vern started in
Kalkaska at the age of 14, worked his
way to Store Mgr. then Advertising.
One of the most creative persons)

Leadership & Spouses enjoying Vern at one
of our Annual Leadership Retreats

• There were other times we celebrated other organizations together.

One example was our annual Bike-a-thon to assist in raising funds for the Michigan Special Olympics. Initially, this started out by associates raising funds to ride from one store to another, starting in Munising located in the northern part of the Upper Peninsula of Michigan on Lake Superior. Those riders would ride to Sault Ste. Marie, which borders the Canada international border, a 120-mile ride (we would have trucks, etc., for assistance along the way). The part of that team with others from the Sault Ste. Marie store would ride to our St. Ignace store, 50 miles away. The next group (normally the largest) would ride from St. Ignace, across the Mackinac Bridge (the world's longest suspended bridge, 5 miles. Obviously, it took connections for the special permits to be able to do this) to our next store along the way, Cheboygan, only 28 miles away, and so it was for a week. After a number of years, we changed our route to a ride from our Gaylord store to Central Michigan University, in Mt. Pleasant, Michigan, the location of the Summer Special Olympics, 103 miles away. It wasn't uncommon to have one hundred riders start the trip. Some would make the whole trip, and most would do a leg (normally about 20 miles at a break) but normally chime in the last leg for the ride into the football field at CMU. Along with having numerous associates volunteer to assist the special Olympians, our group would normally raise over $25,000 to help pay for the Olympians to attend, always second in raising funds to the key sponsor, Spartan Stores.

Needless to say, with this kind of spirit, it goes without being said; our associates responded to countless charities and events in each of our local communities.

Glen's Bike-A-Thon for Special Olympics

On the road for Special Olympics

Glen's Bike-A-Thon for Special Olympics

Glen's Bike-A-Thon for Special Olympics
highlighted in •Off the Shelf•

Presenting the Award is Spartan Store Representative Ron Koets, with Glen Catt and Jim Paterni.

Glen's Markets #1 Retailer!

In 1985 Spartan Stores became the exclusive sponsor of the Special Olympics Summer Games which are held in Mt. Pleasant, Michigan, each June.

Spartan called on its member stores to help promote and support the program. That first year, Glen's Markets did not get very involved.

In 1986, Glen's supported 14 Athletes, one from each of our stores, and had 60 volunteers in Mt. Pleasant to work at the games.

That's when it happened! Those 60 people became hooked on that "Great Feeling" we received in Mt. Pleasant.

In 1987 our store coordinators really got involved and together we raised $12,068, supporting over 300 Athletes, and had 70 Glen's volunteers at the Summer Games. Michigan Special Olympics honored Glen's Markets as the #1 Retail Supporter of 1987. That was an unbelievable accomplishment; one we could only hope to match in 1988.

Glen's Markets receiving an award from Spartan Stores for being the #1 supporting retailer of Special Olympics. A title we kept until we sold the company... thanks to the effort of Jim Paterni, one of our General Merchandise Merchandisers

CHAPTER 5

Our Customer

"Look at Everything You Do From the
Customer's Point of View!"
Cheryl Kester-Jankoviak, Glen's Market
Associate, Cheboygan, Michigan

*A good name is to be more desired than great
wealth, favor is better than silver and gold.*
—Proverbs 22:1

Our customer, although the end focus of what we did at Glen's Markets, was more like the stomach of our business rather than the heart of the business as our associates were. However, if you don't feed the stomach, the head and heart are going to suffer. Trust me, we never discounted our customer. Without a happy, satisfied customer, the best trained and motivated associates are pretty much useless, lost in the dust.

In preparing our associates to want (and that is a key word, "want." It's the bottom line to being self-motivated and to take action, which goes a long way in creating an intentional culture) to take care of our customers' wants and needs, we strived to impress the value of a customer. Back before the turn of the century (boy, that sounds old), when the average household was spending $80–100 a week on groceries, I used to impress upon our associates to vision a tattoo of "$50,000" across a customer's forehead. That would always bring some strange looks. But I would go on to explain that if the average customer spends $80–$100 a week on their family, that would be about $5,000 a year, and if we can keep that customer for ten years, well, you do the math. A customer wasn't worth what was in their shopping cart today; the customer was worth whatever they may spend over their lifetime of shopping with us. And every associate was accountable for doing their part in trying to make that into a very long relationship.

We have all read the line, "The customer is always right. If they are wrong, go back and read the beginning of this statement." An addition that we always added was, "The customer is always right, even if they're wrong, even if they are trying to take advantage of us."

We had a policy that the only associate who was allowed to tell a customer "No!" was a store manager (or, in his absence, the assistant manager). Perhaps this allowed a customer to take advantage of us. Yes, but hey, if they have a potential of spending $50,000 over ten years, isn't it worth it to error on the safe side and not question a good customer until *they* prove themselves wrong?

Besides, and even more importantly, our associates knew that they were now only in the position to say, "Yes!" Hence, we asked them to say the following: "No problem!" "How may I take care of you?"

Do you know the kind of stuff that goes through a customer's head when they feel they are probably going to have to defend the reason they are bringing something back to a store? The uptightness, the second-guessing, the anticipation of the store clerks rebuking, etc. We didn't want to have our associates to be put in the position of defending themselves in that attitude. In fact, we tried to put words in our associate's mouth. We asked that when an associate was approached by a customer with a complaint, with a return, or whatever to have the *first thing* that rolled off their tongue be, "I'm sorry that happened. We are going to take care of that for you with either a replacement or a refund, whichever you would like." Then if they needed to ask any questions about the transaction, the customer has already been assured that their needs or wants were going to be addressed. This not only offered a calm atmosphere for our customer but also gave our associate the ammunition needed to disarm an irritable customer. The last two things we wanted was a customer being concerned about bringing something back and/or one of our associates being the blunt of someone who just needed to kick someone's cat that day. (I never did like that saying anyway.)

I don't know how many times I, and hopefully others in our leadership, repeated the story about the city boy who had a flat tire on a backcountry road late one night. When he went to get his tire out, he realized he did not have a tire iron. Looking down the road, he saw a farmhouse and thought surely a farmer would have a tire iron around his farm. So he started the few hundred-yard walk toward the farm. As he got closer, he started thinking about how early farmers get up in the morning; hence, this farmer was probably already in bed. As he walked a little further, he got thinking how upset this farmer may be for getting woken up so late at night. After all, it was going on midnight. Getting closer to the farmer's front door, he thought how angry this farmer is going to be because some young dude from the city was so careless not to be prepared like farmers are and have all the right equipment in his car. As he almost pounded on the farmer's door, he thought about what a negative situation this was going to be having to face an angry farmer so late at night. When the farmer came to answer the door, the young man just shouted out, "You can just keep your dang tire iron! I can live without it!" And with that, he walked away, leaving the sleepy farmer bewildered as to how he could have helped the young man.

We wanted our associates to be aware that when a customer has something to return or had a negative experience, they are going to come into the store suspecting they are going to be facing a negative challenge in order to get what they feel they needed, and nobody wants angry customers.

I've had numerous customers tell me that as seldom that they ever have to bring anything back, they never felt any animosity because they know they are going to be taken care of. Wow! What's that confidence worth?

Remember the Dotti Snook story I mentioned earlier? When she got home and didn't have all her purchases, our team didn't ask any questions and helped her pick up everything "she felt" she hadn't gotten. She always called Glen's Market "My Glen's!" That's priceless and that was what we strived to develop.

Did we ever get taken advantage of? Sure we did. But we wanted it to become obvious before we would say no to a customer, and again, only the store leadership could do that. If we had the same customer repeatedly bringing things back, then the store manager would be contacted to address it. There were times when we may have even fired a customer.

In our Rose City market, our store manager, Bill Noeske, pointed out a customer to me one day when I was there. He said the "old gent" had a filthy mouth, and every time he went through the checkout, he would say something rude and normally swear at the cashier. Bill said he had one incidence where this gent had brought one of the gals to tears. Obviously, I shared with Bill that was something that he needed to address, but he said firing a customer was something he didn't think he could do, and it was a very rare thing at Glen's. So I introduced myself to the gentleman and told him what I was told. He was a little gruff, so I just told him in a pleasant way that we would certainly never speak to any of our associates that way, and we just couldn't allow others to either. I told him that I really thought there must be something that we were doing wrong to upset him when he shopped with us, so I suggested that he should probably find a different grocery store to shop at. (However, in Rose City, we were the only grocery store, but there was a larger town just twenty minutes away where there were other grocery stores, including another Glen's.) The look on his face from my calm statement surely surprised him as he just said, "Okay," and walked away. Bill said the cashiers hailed me as a hero and that it reinforced that our associates were number one, but as for him, he learned a good lesson that had he addressed it earlier, it may not have resulted in firing a customer (and the associates in his store would have viewed *him* as their hero). A couple of months later when I was in Rose City again, forgetting all about the incident, Bill shared, "Hey, remember Mr.—that you had told him he would probably be more happy shopping somewhere else? Well, now I don't think he shops anyplace else, plus I think he actually goes out of his way to be nice to our cashiers." I guess that just goes to show who knows how some people will respond if you, in a loving and humane way, address a situation.

Cover the basics for your customer, but cover them well, right, and consistently

Please let me kind of repeat that, consistently. I don't know why, but customers will shop at a dirty store; they obviously shop stores with poorly trained clerks, etc. But they shop them because they are consistent, whatever they are.

Service. Even people who go to a discount store, where the store promotes their low overhead because of their basic operation, complain about the service. To most of us, we don't even know how to define "service." A good definition of service was quoted at the beginning of this chapter by one of our associates in our Cheboygan store: Cheryl Kester-Jankoviak, "Look at everything you do from the customer's point of view!" Put differently, "And as you wish that others would do to you, do so to them" (Luke 6:31).

Every set of eyes, every frame of mind, and every human that can enter into a business have their own definition of what service is. And what's interesting is even they can't tell you clearly how they would want to be taken care of. The bottom line is to look at your company from the customer's perspective and then do it before they even know what they need (or more importantly) what they "think" they want. Kudos to Cheryl for remembering that saying, and kudos to Jan Bieske, our store manager there, who must have repeated it numerous times. (Side note on Jan: she was a cashier in one of our other stores, who had been promoted through different positions to her current store manager position because she understood people and valued the wants and the needs of both associates and customers.)

Service is talked about in every business, but there is a big difference between what is preached and what is taught.

Cleanliness. "Cleanliness is next to godliness," Dad would always say. Then he would add, "People will not always notice a clean store, but they will always notice a dirty store." People should just expect that where they purchase their food is from a clean environment.

I have never figured it out, but so often when a business is having financial struggles, due to lack of customer base, the first two things that they tend to attack to help cut expenses is labor (poor service follows) and cleanliness (poor first impression follows). Then they wonder why, even though they have cut costs, their bottom line continues to become even weaker. Perhaps it's not a leadership problem, but rather it's a lack of understanding people and what they, the customer, really want and need, which I guess *is* a leadership problem.

Variety. When is one or two brands of green beans not enough? When your customer wants a different brand or just more options. Okay, maybe green beans are not the right example. How about coffee?

Short story. I was the store manager in our Kalkaska, Michigan, store for nine years in the late sixties and early seventies. During that time, a large amount of crude oil was found in Kalkaska County; hence, a drilling boom took off that lasted for perhaps twenty years. Many of the larger, national oil-related companies built new plants along with the companies that are natural spin-offs of that industry. With that brought a few hundred Texans, Oklahomans, and so on from the southern states. And what was the first thing they were asking for when they came to our store in Kalkaska? Folgers Coffee. I had never even heard of Folgers Coffee. I would repeatedly hear how Folgers Coffee was to die for, and some were saying they were having relatives mailing them cans of coffee from their "homeland" in the South.

Dad always told me, "People are more into what they want than what they need. It was just part of our American culture (and, obviously, is an American blessing for sure). If a customer wants something and we can get it, we need to get it." So I did some research on Folgers Coffee, and this was before we even knew how to spell computer or internet. Calling our main supplier, Spartan Stores Inc., downstate in Grand Rapids, they told me they could not purchase that brand for their Michigan-based retailers but that there was a Spartan retail customer, in Indiana, who was being supplied with Folgers Coffee. I had previously met that retailer before at a Spartan Stores convention, so I called him and worked out a deal where they would purchase a pallet load of one-pound and three-pound cans, in each of the different grinds. Then they would fax us an invoice (we did have fax machines then. Oh, now most readers probably now don't know what a fax machine is). We would transfer the funds to them (actually, they never waited for the funds), and they would place the pallets of coffee on a Spartan truck going back to the warehouse, from which Spartan would then transfer the pallet of coffee to their next truck coming to our store. I really believe that when those southerners came in and saw that huge display of Folgers Coffee, strategically located in the front of the store, news traveled faster than if we had put it on the radio (which Kalkaska didn't have a radio station anyway). Not only was that taking care of customer's wants, it set a great example to our associates and for our (then six stores) as to what extent we needed to go to get a customer what they wanted. (Ironically, thirty years later, Jeanne and I drink Folgers Coffee daily.)

Obviously, there were times when someone might request something that just didn't make sense for us to make room on a shelf because of its uniqueness or perhaps the brand was too much the same to what was already being allocated for shelf space. Then we would offer to get them their product and just sell the case to them at our cost.

Is it impossible to create loyalty?

Marketing gurus today claim there is no such thing as obtaining a "loyal customer." Perhaps, there isn't. But if there is, C. Glen came up with a program that came as close to it as possible.

Like most everything else, there is nothing new in the world, but creative people who use their head for things other than just place a hat on it and see things that give them an idea, and *then they act on it*, and that is the key—they act on it! Dad saw a program in a different grocery organization that gave him an idea. He always desired to give back to the communities that we were in. Often, he would do it in unique ways that most people didn't know, even me. But at times, I would hear of them, like the time he was driving through the tiny town of Alba, just 18 miles away. He saw a group of kids along the road picking up papers and garbage. With them was an adult. Stopping his car, he asked the man what was going on. "This is a youth group from our church. As a positive event, we are picking up along each of the roads coming in and out of our town." With that, Dad reached in his pocket, gave the man some money, and asked him to take the group out for ice cream when they were finished. Then he drove away without giving his name. However, there weren't too many two-toned, blue Lincolns in the area, so the fella was able to do some checking, hence how I heard about it years later. For Dad, this wasn't anything unique. Whenever he could, he would always do things anonymously.

Something that he did that wasn't anonymous was the Glen's Save-Share Program. He took the idea from another retailer, added his mix to it, and then launched it within our (then) six stores. The program was actually quite simple (if you wish to have more people understand something, always word it or organize it in a way so that a fifth grader can understand it). Nonprofit organizations could register (they did not have to have a 501(c)3 filing with the IRS). Once they were registered, they could, by any means they desired (except standing at a Glen's cash register or at one of our front doors), collect the register receipts, add them up, and receive 1% of the total as a donation. The only other stipulation was we requested a minimum reimbursement of $25.00 was required ($2,500 worth of register slips). To assist us in validating the receipts from others and make our receipts more unique, we went to having our cash register receipt paper be green, the same color as our Save-Share logo, and later the Save-Share mascot in our advertising, Greeny Green Slip.

First, 1% doesn't sound like much, but when you consider the average supermarket's after-tax-profit in our country is 1%, that's a pretty staggering commitment. Although some years our bottom line after tax was less than 1%, we strived to do better so most years we were able to beat that industry mark (after all, "average" is either best of the worst or the worst of the best. Think of that the next time you desire to be "average"). Speaking of the accounting end of the business, the typical advertising for a grocery store was also about 1%. With us having six locations at that time, each sharing the same printed advertising, we were able to budget our advertising and promotions below the national level. Hence, you might say the cost of the Save-Share Program came out of our advertising budget, which is actually what we did. After a short time, Save-Share became the number one avenue for countless organizations in northern Michigan to raise funds.

Let me share a couple of brief stories that were not untypical. Gaylord had, and still does have, a very large Catholic population. We had numerous associates, and customers tell us that when Msgr. Kaminski, the current father at the local parish (now with the Lord), spoke about giving each Sunday, as they passed the offering, he used to kiddingly (I'm assuming) say, "Now, I don't want to hear any clinging of change, and I want to see a lot of those green receipts in there." Although he never mentioned Glen's Market, we were the only store with a green cash register receipt. Way back then in the early seventies, the Gaylord Catholic Parish was annually collecting over $25,000.00 through the Glen's Save-Share Program, quite a sum in the 1970s.

Fred Armstrong, then our store manager in Grayling, shared the story that one night when he was home, some Boy Scouts came to his door and said they were collecting "green slips." Fred, being the character he is, said, "What are those?" The boys replied, "Those are the cash register receipts from Glen's Market. We collect them to help cover the costs of our troop." From which, Fred said, "Oh, I don't shop there." For which, their reply was, "Gee, you should! It's a really great place, and they help us a lot with the green slips." Hence, Fred fessed up and went and found some green slips for them.

I am not sure if anyone knows how many dollars we ended up sharing back to our communities, but we did celebrate the year that we were able to share $1 million for that year to organizations. That would have resulted in $100 million in cash register receipts coming back to us. That takes loyalty on the customer's part. And the program just kept growing. They say the best kind of advertising is word of mouth. Precisely, that was how Save-Share grew.

I'll let you decide if this was a loyalty program or an opportunity to find a fair way to share back to our communities or perhaps both.

Glen's Save-Share logo

1983 SAVE-SHARE HONOR ROLL
Group & organizations that have shared at least $250.00

$1,250,000

GAYLORD SAVE-SHARE HONOR ROLL

St. Mary's Cathedral School	$1,505.32
St. Mary's (Cathedral)	$4,340.93
Jehovah's Witnesses	$437.23
South Maple School/P.T.O./Annex	$2,735.49
Area Cub/Boy Scouts	$1,058.22
Community Child Care Center	$258.45
RLDS Church/Womens' Dept.	$312.76
Zonta	$312.76
Evangelical Free Church	$273.89
St. Thomas Church	$535.56
Area Brownie/Girl Scouts	$840.37
Assembly of God Church	$373.18
Joburg-Lewiston Senior Class	$983.01
Otsego County Library	$800.45
Otsego County Sr. Citz. Housing Ass'n	$538.57
Northern Mich. Comm. Mental Health Brd.	$360.63
Peace Lutheran Church	$516.90
Gaylord Band Boosters	$373.83
Gaylord High School Wrestling Team	$571.53
Waters/Gaylord Lioness Club	$334.13
First United Methodist Church	$537.48
Eagles Auxiliary	$329.07
Otsego Lake Baptist Church	$302.33
North Ohio P.T.O.	$3,064.36
Otsego Memorial Hospital Auxiliary	$404.80
Gaylord Community Church	$249.84
Congregational Church	$270.22
Calvary Baptist Church	$948.81
Otsego Country Day School	$398.70
Vanderbilt Community Church	$308.69

KALKASKA SAVE-SHARE HONOR ROLL

Kalkaska Sunshine Guild	$555.68
Church of Christ Sunshine Guild	$447.91
ABC Nursery	$561.52
Garfield Athletic Club	$284.06
New Life Assembly	$351.95
Bethany Circle, People's Church	$562.97
Area T.O.P.S. Clubs	$381.63
Evergreen Baptist Bible Church	$594.67
Kalk. High School Class of '83	$1,218.49
Kalk. Varsity Cheerleaders	$373.56
Kalk. Comm. Nutrition Program	$402.33
Kalkaska Jehovah's P.T.O.	$1,020.45
Kalkaska Hospital Auxiliary	$343.54
Forest Area High School Class of '83	$660.41
Kalk. Girls' Basketball Program/Team	$358.84
Lions' Club - Sunrise	$295.69
Bear Lake Fire Dept.	$265.30
Boy Scouts Troop #9	$257.19
Spencer Church of Christ	$276.83
St. Paul's Ladies Guild	$407.84

GRAYLING SAVE-SHARE HONOR ROLL

Grayling Co-op Nursery	$366.22
St. John's Lutheran Church Women	$262.56
Grayling Middle School Science	$658.37
Middle School Resource Room	$1,254.18
St. Mary's Altar Society	$574.78
G H S Wrestling Team	$340.00
R.S.V.P.	$418.16
Mt. Hope Lutheran Church	$591.68
St. Francis Epis. Church Altar Soc.	$345.42
Grayling High Class of '83	$553.60
Grayling Senior Citizens	$408.67
Area Brownie/Girl Scouts	$518.75
Area Cub/Boy Scouts	$813.56
Hospital Auxiliary	$377.70
Lovell's Community Sunday School	$324.05
Free Methodist Church	$376.11
Grayling Lioness Club	$269.24
Frederic Community Library	$433.29
Grayling Elementary	$1,971.75
Frederic Elementary	$463.39

MIO SAVE-SHARE HONOR ROLL

Mio Church of God	$418.74
Mio Co-op Nursery	$474.08
Mio Wesleyan Church	$260.83
V.F.W. Aux. Post #4126	$354.66
Amer. Legion Aux. (Walley Bartley)	$281.63
Fairview Class of 1984	$1,420.50
Mio School Class of '83	$1,183.86
Mio St. Mary's	$1,001.07
Knights of Columbus	$455.51
Luzerne Fire Dept.	$266.03
Mio Animal Shelter	$349.92
Seventh Day Adventist Church	$1,115.14
Women of the Moose	$632.75
St. Bartholemew's Episcopal Church	$450.87
Mio-AuSable Music Boosters	$315.21
Emma Lowery United Church of Christ	$252.72
United Methodist Church	$549.80
Oscoda County Library	$303.29
Fairview 10th Grade	$329.86
Mio Men of the Moose	$325.44
Mio Elementary School	$3,212.76

CHARLEVOIX SAVE-SHARE HONOR ROLL

St. Mary's School	$1,200.22
Ellsworth Schools	$914.02
Charlevoix Co-op Nursery	$618.09
Charlevoix Schools	$3,378.47
Area Girl Scouts	$224.66
Bethany Lutheran Church	$465.44
Childrens' Place	$737.25
CHS Speech Team	$328.16
Community Church of God Sr. High Youth	$344.61
Central Lake 6th Grade (Porath)	$553.40
Charlevoix County Humane Society	$1,878.92
Ironton Congregational Church	$349.02

ROSE CITY SAVE-SHARE HONOR ROLL

Ogemaw District Library	$1,478.27
Rose City Schools	$3,089.99
Rose City Co-op Nursery	$737.14
Prince of Peace Lutheran Women	$257.27
Area Girl Scouts	$422.66
Lupton Friends Church Youth Group	$286.98
Lioness Club	$431.92
Lupton Area Senior Citizens	$798.11
St. John's Lutheran Church	$1,173.78
Rose City Trail Blazers	$371.24

WEST BRANCH SAVE-SHARE HONOR ROLL

St. Helen Retirees Club	$261.47
Surline Elementary School	$3,737.11
Awana Youth Association	$1,461.52
Moose Lodge/Women of the Moose	$286.56
Area Girl Scouts	$422.66
West Branch Schools	$811.66
Peter Pan Pre-School	$479.41
Skidway Lake Senior Citizen Center	$546.33
Surline Middle School	$1,744.43
St. Joseph's Church	$2,458.09
Holy Family Church/Altar Soc./Parish	$280.43
Churchill United Methodist Church/Women	$512.21
Spring Hill Association	$270.79
W.B. Area Rhythm Riders Club	$274.61
RLDS Church	$342.44
Trinity Episcopal Church	$297.93
Free United Methodist Church	$718.02

KEEP SAVIN'
THOSE GREEN SLIPS!

"Greenie"

TO HAVE GREENIE GREENSLIP
VISIT YOUR GROUP OR
ORGANIZATION, CONTACT YOUR
LOCAL GLEN'S STORE MANAGER
FOR DETAILS.

ROGERS CITY SAVE-SHARE HONOR ROLL

P.I.A.R.C. (Hawk's Center)	$876.48
St. John's Lutheran School	$2,365.23
St. John's Lutheran Church	$1,121.04
P I County Council on Aging	$956.39
Westminster Jr. High Youth Fellowship	$447.76
St. Ignatius School	$2,497.31
R.C. Womens' Softball Association/	
Baseball League	$319.67
Presque Isle Library	$346.46
Faith Evangelical Lutheran Church	$377.02
Area Brownies/Girl Scouts	$272.03
R.C. Spanish Club	$330.36
Big Bros./Big Sisters	$330.39
St. Dominic's Parish	$418.10
St. Michael's Lutheran Church	$303.13
N.E.M.A. EMT's	$685.68
Immanuel Lutheran Church	$438.32

MANCELONA SAVE-SHARE HONOR ROLL

Antrim County Senior Citizens Center	$433.47
Lakes of the North Ecology Community	$278.95
Mancelona Business Girls	$492.37
St. Anthony's Guild	$697.50
Mancelona WMS Missionary Church	$375.02
Alba Elementary School	$1,817.30
United Methodist Women	$440.23
Mancelona Twp. Library	$476.68
Unsung Heroes	$3,078.42
Area Girl Scouts	$539.69
King's Kids Youth Group Camp	$553.92
Mancelona Lions	$261.69
Women of the Moose	$652.04
Kids Fish Pond	$272.76
MHS Band	$322.76
Mancelona Cheerleaders	$311.55
Mancelona Medical Center	$570.11

ROSCOMMON SAVE-SHARE HONOR ROLL

Gerrish/Higgins Fire Dept.	$292.88
First Congregational Church	$1,242.23
Roscommon Senior Citizens	$447.38
Area Cub/Boy Scouts	$393.25
Golden Angel's Club	$375.86
Roscommon Co-op Nursery	$365.92
Area Brownie/Girl Scouts	$775.22
Roscommon Baptist Church	$342.80
COOR T.M.I./II	$557.54
Girls' Varsity Basketball Team	$446.41
St. Michael's Religious Education	$474.81
Roscommon Youth Baseball League	$293.01

EAST JORDAN SAVE-SHARE HONOR ROLL

E.J. Athletic Boosters	$1,625.84
E.J. Sen. Citz. Center/Advisory Council	$368.17
E.J. Learning Center	$383.17
Silver Spurs 4-H	$263.91
Church of Everlasting God	$878.98
Missionary Church	$1,001.34
St. Joseph's Church	$1,168.83
Area Girl Scouts	$523.03
E J. Elementary School	$2,605.67
St. John's Church	$333.50
RLDS Church	$457.23
First Presbyterian Church	$422.80
Jehovah's Witnesses	$359.18
E.J. Public Library	$945.43
Evangelical Lutheran Church	$253.08
Area Cub Scouts/Boy Scouts	$587.73
E.J. Womens' Softball League	$960.31
Charlevoix County 4-H	$546.26
Ebenezer Christian School	$428.91
E.J. Cheerleaders	$1,151.13
E.J. Indian Class (Nelson)	$273.42
E.J. Lioness Club	$1,463.17
E.J. Co-op Nursery	$418.08

HOUGHTON LAKE SAVE-SHARE HONOR ROLL

St. James CCW	$573.24
United Methodist Church	$1,002.59
Seventh Day Adventist Church	$286.80
DOES #149	$393.47
H.L. Wesleyan Church	$611.18
Prudenville Student Club	$276.72
Markey Baptist Missionary Church Soc.	$326.54
Assembly of God	$312.37
Messiah Lutheran Church Women	$302.98
Our Lady of the Lake Church	$334.37
Our Lady of the Lake School	$677.40
H.L. Cub/Boy Scouts	$362.08
H.L. Varsity Softball	$257.38
St. John's Lutheran Church	$359.10
Houghton Lake Third Grade Class	$306.21

One of our Save-Share newsletters that we distributed to customers announcing some more active organizations

Picture of •Greenie• and a little boy

Some Consider These Real Collector's Items

WHEN MY FATHER, C. Glen Catt, started **Save-Share** in 1972, "giving back" to the community was a pretty novel concept for a retailer. But here at Glen's Markets, **Save-Share** has become a symbol of great accomplishment for us. It not only demonstrates our sincere sense of obligation to the communities we serve, it reflects the dedicated patronage and confidence our customers have in us.

OVER THE YEARS, hundreds of northern Michigan organizations have qualified to participate in the **Save-Share** program. From Girl Scouts to Hospice, from elementary schools to area churches, organizations receive one percent of each cash register receipt collected on their behalf. In this way, Glen's Markets is able to give back to each community in a most meaningful and productive manner.

THE **SAVE-SHARE** PROGRAM has just hit the $8 million mark. It's difficult to imagine that those little green receipts could add up so quickly. We deeply appreciate the thousands of Glen's Markets customers who have made it all possible, and are proud to share in their many volunteer endeavors that, collectively, make our community a better place to live.

Marketing even talked me into promoting Save-Share, which I was proud to do...

*Create a destination place where a customer wants
what you have but can only get it from you.*

I am sure I cannot relay each of the areas that we strived to accomplish this, but I will share a few.

In the story about Dottie Snook, she came into Glen's Market to purchase her food but also to pick up some sweatshirts and warmer clothes that they hadn't brought up from downstate yet. At the time, Walmarts weren't heard of in our area, and we didn't have any K-marts in northern Michigan at the time either. There were a few, small Ben Franklin stores. For those who may not be familiar with them, they were the most current style of the old 5- and 10-cent stores. Oh, probably none of you remember those. They were a variety store and they did carry some clothing at the time. Glen's carried a variety of clothing because one, they weren't readily available in the towns we were in, and second, with gross profit margins of 30–40 percent, they were a whole lot more profitable than groceries, although the turns (the number of times a product runs through its shelf inventory in a year) were very low.

(Side note: In a grocery store, turns are very important. It is much more profitable to have an item that only carries a 16 percent gross but turns fifty-two times a year {weekly} than to have an item that carries a 40 percent gross but only turns two to three times a year. You can do the math.)

Hence, back when there weren't many clothing options, Glen's offered the convenience and destination for some clothing items.

We got heavier into greeting cards because the local drugstores (only locations to carry cards at the time) had limited displays. As you can see, many things have changed over the years, so we continued to be flexible.

One of the areas that we always pride ourselves on was our meat departments. When the supply of product that we had available to us from our wholesaler seemed to be just the "okay," about the same as every other food retailer in our area, we took a different approach. Our (then) director of meats, John Rolfe (remember the kid in the Grayling meat department who said he someday wanted Mr. Taylor's job?), heard about a small group of independent stores who had formed a co-op. They had created a group who worked directly with cattle ranchers in the West and Midwest, contracted them to raise a breed of cattle for them, and then contracted slaughterhouses to prepare the beef the way they wanted it and having USDA inspectors grade the beef so that only their standards would be shipped to their stores. Any beef that did not meet their standards would be sold on the open market to others.

Being able to join this organization allowed us to offer a "Glen's Brand" of beef, consistently with the quality that we determined. In our markets, it was a superior product and became a destination item for our customer. They couldn't get it anyplace else, and it was really quality stuff, and we could market within pennies per pound of what we had been purchasing.

In marketing the new beef program to our leadership and meat department managers, we flew our managers and meat managers west to tour a couple of the ranchers, meeting the ranchers themselves. And we visited slaughterhouses and literally watched USDA inspectors approve beef for Glen's Markets (stamping our logo on the side of the quarter hanging beef) and rejecting the product that did not meet our standard (stamping "choice" or "good" on the side of the quarter to be sold to other retailers).

Perhaps out of the many, many destination items we adopted, the President's Choice was one of the most successful, if not the most.

I had mentioned Brian Whitman, who we had recruited from a much larger east coast chain of stores. Brian had become our VP of marketing by now. He was aware of and now introduced us to the President's Choice brand. No one in Michigan was carrying this product. In fact, the distribution was extremely exclusive and highly controlled by the creator of the label, which was Loblaw Companies Limited of Canada.

President's Choice was more commonly known by its logo as PC. In a nutshell, the parent company of PC traveled the world to find the best quality of any one product. They would contract it and then have it packaged under their private label of President's Choice.

I kid you not, it is excellent stuff, mostly food items but also many nonfood items.

Brian was able to obtain some of the product for us to sample. Quite honestly, it sounded and tasted too good to be true. If we could obtain this product line, one, we would be the only ones in Michigan to carry it; two, it was as good or in most cases superior to any national brands that we carried (or anyone else); three, we could offer it at a retail below national brand pricing (and in most cases lower than what we were selling our wholesaler's private label brand); and four, even at the lower retail, our percentage of profit was much higher. Like I said, it all sounded way too good to be true. But we had developed enough confidence in Brian that we were open to pursue it. The bigger challenge was our company, even with two dozen stores now, we were smaller than any other company that Loblaw had allowed to carry this exclusive product. And, of course, there was the challenge of getting distribution to each of our rural stores. As it was, we had recently built and opened our own little 50,000-square-foot distribution center with the intent of purchasing items with limited special pricing so that we could offer our consumers a better value. Plus we had also recently purchased a fleet of tractors and trailers to haul that product, along with all of our nonrefrigerated purchases from Spartan Stores in Grand Rapids.

The Loblaw headquarters was located in Toronto, Canada, and Brian was able to arrange a meeting with their top leadership who oversaw the PC product. Now, it was up to us to tell the Glen's Market's story and see if we could sell ourselves.

For those who are not aware of the air travel limitations in northern Michigan, we contracted a local charter, North Country Aviation. Although it may not have been the smartest thing in the world to do (due to the repercussions to the company, had that plane had cracked up), we took our top eight leaders and flew from Gaylord directly to Toronto. We must have put on the boondock charm and displayed our enthusiasm as when we left, we were sure they were as excited about working with us as we were with them.

Over the next few months, we were able to work out the details where the PC product was delivered to our warehouse located in the town of Waters (about eight miles south of Gaylord but right next to I-75 entrance and on/exit ramps). Within just over a year, the roughly fifty President's Choice products we were carrying started accounting for 10 percent of our total dry grocery sales. Our customers were raving about the PC product, *and they couldn't get it anywhere else.*

Obviously, we took advantage of the name and made it personal even with myself, reluctantly, agreeing to appear in our advertising as the President's Choice. Our marketing team even convinced me to do a photo op with our Old English sheepdog, Muffin. That advertisement continued to haunt me by those who knew me. First, everyone knew I didn't care for dogs, and Muffin and I never had become close mates. Second, Muffin had numerous health challenges; hence, she was on special dog food, of which even that had to have enzymes added to it twenty minutes prior to serving it to her. I made sure that even though the insinuation was there, nowhere in the advertisement did it actually say that Muffin consumed President's Choice dog food.

I have quoted that my dad would say if you want to be successful in business, evaluate what people need and want and what's missing, so that never left our minds. And we tried different things.

One of those that wasn't too successful was putting RadioShack franchises in some of our stores back in the mid-seventies. This started in Kalkaska after we had added onto the building. We had some extra space, so I looked for something to fill it. Being the store manager at the time, I knew our town didn't have anything to offer the expanding electronics interest (this was in the mid-1970s). I contacted RadioShack, and although they had never put a franchise in a grocery store, they agreed, and Dad agreed to let me try it. It must have taken off pretty good at first as between our, then, six stores, we ended up having three RadioShack franchises, although they were pretty short-lived as they really didn't pan out.

Many years later, in the early 1990s, we were putting a major addition on our Gaylord location, taking it to what would have been probably the largest supermarket in the north at the time.

The Gaylord community had been without a Dairy Queen for over twenty-five years, the closest one being about 35 miles away, a trip I was all too familiar with as DQs were a family favorite. My wife, Jeanne, said, "You are always looking for destination products, you should put a Dairy Queen in the addition." Now, that was new for me! So we, roughly, drew one into the building plans, and I called the Dairy Queen Corporate Headquarters and asked about a franchise. I got a pretty quick "no interest." Not giving up very easily, I called the headquarters back and asked for the president's office. It is funny that most people think that the president of a company should be hands off or above everyone, but Dad always taught me that everyone puts their pants on the same way, and a title just reflects the level of accountability. It's also always interesting to me that most often when you ask to be transferred to the president's office, they do just that, without asking any further questions. "Well, that's an interesting concept" was his reply when we finally connected. "We have never had a franchise in a grocery store before."

"Always a first time," I said. "We have it designed in the front corner of the building so that we could have a drive up. Could I send you a copy of our concept plans?" A week later, I received a call from the DQ president (sorry I do not remember his name). He asked if I could be available if he had their corporate plane fly into Otsego County Airport (he had already had his pilot check the size of the airport). Two weeks later, with the two of us sitting in my office and with the plans spread out on the floor, he agreed to sell us a franchise. By the way, the Gaylord Dairy Queen was a success, made a profit the first year, and is still open to this day—no more drives out of town for our family to get a DQ treat anymore.

Something else that was beginning to be popular was specialty coffees. It was another element that our customers driving downstate could experience but they couldn't experience in northern Michigan. Starbucks was gaining name popularity; however, for us, the closest was over two hundred miles away.

In our design for the Gaylord addition, we penciled in a spot for a coffee shop. I contacted the regional Starbucks office and asked about getting a franchise. Although Starbucks now has both corporate operated stores and franchised stores on about every corner and in countless retail stores, in the early 1990s, they told me that they were not doing franchises yet. Okay, knowing that I was just looking for something that would be a destination department (and assuming that the coffee business probably wasn't all that profitable. Wow, what I didn't know), I asked if I could send a copy of our concept plans for the area we had drawn into our addition. If they could consider putting a corporate store inside our store, I would offer them a five-year lease for one dollar a year. My theory would be I would have a Starbucks destination puller, and I may not be making any dollar return on that space in the store, but then again, I wouldn't have the equipment investment and the labor and, more than likely, wouldn't also experience the loss expected in the first few years of getting that business going. Although the individual I spoke to was intrigued, when she called me back, she said the offer was interesting, but because of the costs of getting the product to only one location "way up north," they would have to pass.

Funny side note, there is now a Starbucks franchise in the exact location in the Gaylord store that we had proposed almost thirty years ago.

I share these stories because they are some of the, behind the scenes, actions that we took to be unique in offering our consumer some excitement in an otherwise boring week-to-week shopping duty.

Get to know and understand your customer

As I shared with getting to know our associates, we strived to understand our customers too.

Within our industry, reward (or loyalty) cards were starting to be introduced. When I came back from one of my trips visiting larger retailers around the country, I introduced the idea to our marketing team. To say the least, Brian Whitman was somewhat familiar with loyalty cards as Harris Teeter had just started to put a card together about the time he was leaving.

Through some great research of the different software available at the time, the development and the marketing of the Glen's Card became a great success. By encouraging our customer base to use the card, we could treat our customers reflective to their shopping habit at Glen's. (Obviously, the revolution of store loyalty cards has expanded a lot since then.) Some examples are as follows:

- By using the card, they could receive special pricing that was reflected via shelf signs.
- Based on their loyalty, we would send flyers to their address to reward them for shopping with us. For example, at Thanksgiving, most retailers sell turkeys at or below their cost (don't ask me why; we just did). However, though we priced our turkeys competitively, in our mailings to our Glen's Card customer base, we would include a coupon. To our most loyal customers (based on their purchases), they would receive a coupon for a free turkey. For the next level of loyal customer, they might receive a coupon for five dollars off their Thanksgiving Turkey, etc. We would do this for other products throughout the year in our monthly Glen's Card mailings. We would hear of customers who told other customers why they got a better coupon because they were more loyal.

This helped us realize that for years, we have been sending out thousands of printed advertisements and offering at cost or below cost specials, and although our loyal customers would get the deals, we had also been rewarding the "bargain shopper," who would go from store to store to just shop the deals. Bottom line, we realized we were losing money on the bargain shoppers and making all our profit (plus having to make up the loss from the bargain hunters) from our loyal customers. With the Glen's Card, we could reward our loyal customers while still offering the bargain shopper to get our specials with the card, but not the loyalty bonuses, which we offered plenty.

• There were numerous things we could do and did do with the card, which I won't go into. But one thing we did, which really opened the eyes to our leadership teams, was rewarding our top loyalty customers at CHRISTmas. Around the first of December, each of our store managers would receive a list of their top twenty-five loyalty customers for the year. From that list, they would put together a really special fruit/gift basket, and they, along with the assistant store manager, would personally take the gift to those customer's homes to thank them for being such a loyal customer that year.

I have no idea who came up with that idea (we had such an awesome and dedicated marketing team), but the real value that came out of this wasn't necessarily the reward to our top twenty-five customers in each store. The real eye-opener was that our store team realized that many of the gifts they were delivering were going to persons living in, well, not the nicest neighborhoods. In fact, many of their top shoppers were those living in mobile homes.

This opened our eyes to the fact that those on limited incomes were, much often, less likely to eat in restaurants and ate most all their meals at home, as compared to the growing public that had been eating out more often.

(Side note: As I write this, we are in the midst of the COVID-19 pandemic. For the past three months, grocery stores have not been able to keep up with the added business from people not being able to eat in restaurants. To compound that, many of the grocery store's suppliers and manufacturers cannot keep up with the demand because they are different suppliers/manufacturers that have been supplying restaurants. It is surprising to see the "aha" on people's faces when I've been able to help them understand why their grocery store cannot keep their shelves stocked. Our family still owns about half the stores [real estate] that Spartan purchased the business, so we are privy to their sales; in many cases, they are close to double. It's a nice problem to have if you can get the product.)

Another note that I would like to include is the confidentiality that our marketing team placed on individual purchases. No one was to be allowed to go into the system and search what a customer was purchasing. At one point, I was curious if a classmate of mine, in one of the towns we had a store, was a customer of ours. So I asked Stan Dziki if he would check to see what their purchases were. Stan's reply was that we do not allow anyone to go into the system to pinpoint one customer's purchases. If being the president, that was something that I wished to pursue, I would have to make my request to Brian Whitman. I remember walking away, thankful for the integrity, but feeling a little sheepish that I had asked.

Friendliness comes automatically with the right culture

Remember my earlier comment? "Happy associates create happy customers."

One might think it is easy to create a friendly atmosphere for your customers. However, nothing is more from the truth. As a business leader, you can preach friendliness, friendliness, friendliness until you are blue in the face, but people still have their own personal baggage when they come to work and put their name tag on. And now you are suggesting you put this monkey on their shoulders that they have to put on a happy face because the business wants them to.

As humans, we take joy in what we are doing when we can help others smile.

Obviously, those in leadership were to set the standard in creating a positive, happy atmosphere. But intentionally creating a positive culture involves more than trying to paint on a happy face.

In "viewing everything you do from the customer's point of view," here are just a few things that we would share:

- Perhaps your contact with an elder customer may be the only people contact that they will have that day. What can each of us do to brighten their day?
- Most customers are on a budget. Shopping and trying to stretch their budget is not the most exciting thing to do. What can we do to help lighten that burden?
- Watch a customer's eyes smile if you compliment them on something or on their child.
- What are your personal struggles when you go grocery shopping? How would you rather be treated?

When we, with our human nature, see the responses and the difference we can make in a customer's attitude, it is always reflected back on ourselves in our attitude. I wish I could actually quote what spouses have shared with me about their spouse's attitude after a day's work at Glen's as compared to when they "used" to come home from working somewhere else. The truth is it really wasn't us at Glen's. Oh, we may have pointed it out, but when we shoot a smile toward someone else, it normally always comes ricocheting back at us. We actually become the recipient of our own positive attitude.

Of course, pricing is always a key to customer service

Although being competitive goes without question, people remember the quality much longer than they will remember the price. I heard that echoed from my dad countless times. People remember quality or, more so, lack of quality.

"Many businesses claim to be the lowest priced, but no one can be the lowest on everything. The grocery business works on volume, and it is extremely competitive. With such a low margin, many retailers have tried to be the lowest priced on most everything, only to price themselves out of business."

As typical in the grocery business, we would watch the top-selling four to five hundred items in the market price accordingly and then price other items based on their movement and demand, constantly watching the change in shopping demands and habits. Miracle Whip used to be one of the highest turn items in the stores. It would always be priced well below our cost (sometimes, I question the sanity of a grocer). But now, with people more health conscious, that product is no longer kept track of. Another item of example is a five-pound bag of sugar, but now the standard question I hear from housewives is, "Who bakes anymore?" (My Jeanne does.)

Honestly, we didn't consider pricing as a customer service but more of being conscious of being competitive with other supermarkets. We didn't play it down, but we didn't play it up either. We did run some great advertised specials (most often below our cost), but the statistics always claimed that less than 10 percent of the public shop advertisements.

> *If you're competitor focused, you have to wait until there is a competitor doing something. Being customer focused allows you to be more pioneering.*
> —Jeff Bezos, Founder of Amazon.com

CHAPTER 6

Additional Intentional Philosophies in the Glen's Culture

Intentional leadership

Everything starts with having a reason and a purpose of doing it. *Wandering generalities* never find their mark and almost always end up falling off a mountain somewhere.

Intentional leadership is not allowing things to just happen. It is focusing on the purpose and not on the preferences. Let me repeat that: purpose over preferences. Intentional leadership is about being intentional in everything that you do. Let me repeat that also: Intentional leadership is about being intentional in *everything* that you do.

It's about being on top of understanding what you are doing, what's old but still working, what's new that may work better than how it has been/being done, and what is best for your unique situation, for your culture, for your associates, for your customers, and for your stockholders.

It's about being aware of your associates and who they are as individuals, realizing that they have aspirations too, however different they may be than yours. They have 24-7 lives: families, friends, interests, talents, successes, failures, struggles, etc. We each have our circle of life; at some point, we overlap, but only there is where our connection is. They have a whole another life going on out there, and as their employer, we need to be ever conscious of that if we desire to build a strong relationship and recreating culture.

It's about knowing your customer's needs, wants, and desires. Who is your customer? What can you and your team do to have them consider you being their supplier of what they want, and to get them to say, "I wouldn't go anyplace else!" What worked yesterday may work today, but it may not either. What works today may be good, but is there a better way or product that you can offer? Where is your industry going tomorrow? With what you know, do you think it is the right direction? If you are not sure, what are you doing about it to educate yourself so that you can decide if you want to head that way or not?

In the Bible, God mentions *today* in many different ways, but what He is saying is "Today is a new day. You cannot change yesterday. You cannot do anything about tomorrow. Today is the element of time that you have for sure, do with it what you can, and then let tomorrow become another day. Every day is new."

The age-old saying "Plan your work then work your plan" means just that. You look at every element of your business or organization:

- What are the results that you desire to accomplish in each element of your business and the totality of the unit?
- How do you truly desire to take care of your associates? What is the level of value that they play in your equation?
- At what lengths will you go to take care of your customer? Are profits more important? Are sales more important? Or are they realized as the end result/success in how your customer has been taken care of?
- Are you focused on the long range or short range? (*Family businesses* focus on the long picture; hence, they can easily make decisions about associates and customers ahead of the bottom line. *Large corporations* have a tendency to focus on the short term; hence, bureaucracy within the system forces decisions based on weekly, monthly, or quarterly

results, normally not advantageous for customers nor associates alike.)

- Do you just focus on what you are doing right or always evaluate your weaknesses with the intent of improving each little element?
- Do you put together a business plan or a vision plan, evaluate it often, communicate it, and stick to it? And do you bring other key people into putting it together—"those who help plan the trip enjoy the ride most."

This list could go on and on. I know we didn't have all the answers, and if we were still in business today, we still wouldn't. Any business or organization that involves people, people's lives, and the circle of society that we live in needs to know that the target is ever moving.

With that said, I like a quote by Aristotle, "While everything changes, everything remains the same as well." With technology and the pace of people's lives being thrown into it because of it, we need to continue to strive to ride the edge on change. On the other hand, people are people; they have always, and still have needs and wants. Watching the change of attitudes over the years, people's wants have long started to outweigh their needs. That goes for associates, that goes for customers, and that goes for investors. Good leaders and great leaders can balance this. They have to balance this.

Below, I am going to touch on some of the intentional elements that, at Glen's Markets, we strived to ride herd on. They obviously do not cover all the bases, but like the heart of this book, the purpose is to share the Glen's Market's story and hope that in the process, you (as a leader) may find something that you can take and make a difference from it. Dad always told me if I go to a seminar and realize one thing that I wish to do differently, it was well worth the time.

An intentional culture recreates itself

It stands to reason that the more people on your team, whether you call them associates, members, employees, etc., that buy in and live the intended culture, the more impact it is going to have on other associates and likewise on your customers and your financial results, like the example I had given earlier of the seasoned high school bagger/carryout correcting a new cashier that they were associates not employees.

The more you, as leaders, talk and (more importantly) live the intended culture, the more it is going to rub off on the rest of the team. Obviously, this includes every time, let me repeat that, *every time you* witness something contrary to the intended culture, you correct it. But make sure you correct it in a positive, culture-driven way. Likewise, when you witness an action that reinforces the culture, call attention to it, and compliment it.

Your competition cannot duplicate your culture, and you should have the kind of culture that you would not want to duplicate theirs.

Personal example

You may have over two thousand associates as we did, or you may have three. You cannot personally be watching them all the time, but I assure you they are watching you all the time, even the ones who have never met you or even ever laid eyes on you. Trust me, when you, as the leader (not necessarily the president or so-called higher echelon but one of the leaders in their mind), do something out of culture, news travels fast. "I know this is the way that we are supposed to do things at Glen's, but I saw Glen do—(or heard that Glen did—). So, I guess it's probably okay to do sometimes." You do not need that kind of gossip.

I shared it earlier in this book, but I will share it again. Leading by example is the number one element to create a superior culture, a superior team, superior customers, and superior results. Is that tough? You bet it is. It is like living in a glasshouse. My dad used to say, "If you always tell the truth, you never have to wonder what you said." It's the same for being a living example of what you believe (and preach). If you always live and act that way, you never have to wonder who is watching, and trust me, there is always somebody watching!

Intentional hiring practices

Again, I credit Bill Brown, at Glen's Markets, for really pushing this when the hiring pool was low.

Now, before I get on this spiel, let me state that because the way a person looked, their gender, their skin color, their nationality, or their choice of religion whether they were hired or not, was never a factor. An individual's education (or lack of) or their history (unless it involved dishonesty) was also never a factor.

Obviously, experience could play a big factor in the position that they may be hired for. But attitude, positiveness, eye contact, and showing an interest in people were the key traits that we looked for. We could teach and train those with a lack of experience. Numerous times the down-and-out with a great attitude would be capable to rise to leadership positions if given the training and the opportunity and being treated like the God-created human that they were.

With that said, we all know companies that hire individuals who just have a pulse and then give them a little training. Go ahead, I'm sure you can name one (and you can name a number of them who are no longer in business because of it). History is full of those companies that were once a great company but then crumbled because of poor decisions, starting with their hiring practices. K-mart is probably one of the most well-known.

Expect your leadership, especially upper management, to replicate your beliefs, and expect them to expect their immediates to do the same

If you deviate from this one iota, the watered-down effect on others in the organization will make your intentional beliefs, standards, values, etc., whitewashed to the tenth degree. At Glen's, we had the standards that I have previously laid out in this book, and we expected our team to not just agree with them and not just live with them but to digest them and enhance them anywhere they could.

That being said, Denny and I were both outspoken born-again Christians. We did not hide that; however, we did not expect those we worked with to have to follow our belief in Jesus, although many did. But with our Christian beliefs came our standards, our values, and our morals that we incorporated into our business because, well, it was the right thing to do. It resulted in treating associates right and customers right, and it guided us to always strive to make the truest and most honest decisions that we were capable of.

There were times we had associates who were exceptionally productive and produced awesome (sales and financial) results, but they felt that their way of handling associates and some of their shady decisions was more important to obtain the results. You know the saying "one bad apple"; thus, when the truth would float to the top, which it always did, they would become history at Glen's. Would we *fire* them? Not necessarily. But in respect for the job they had done, we would give them a timeline and suggest they seek other employment. This fits in with Dad's statement of always being "firm but fair."

The culture becomes successful only if everyone embraces it.

Be intentional and consistent with all communications

I have already shared that I truly believe that you can never overcommunicate. Communicate, communicate, communicate! If you are communicating positive things, especially about people, put it on paper. You would be surprised how many people share something positive about them that was in writing. I have witnessed people show me notes that I had written to them (or about them) years prior that they had continued to hang on to. In fact, just this week, Jeanne pulled out some notes that I have saved over thirty-five years from a seminar we had put on for management where we asked participants to write other associates a brief note on how you felt about them. These were notes that others had written about me, and nope, I never threw them away.

On the other hand, if you have something that needs to be addressed that is negative, or even constructive, do not send it in writing, but do it verbally, in person (best), or by phone, and never, never in front of another individual, unless it is important that you have a witness.

People, associates, and customers like to be kept informed

I always liked Zig Ziglar's statement, "Those who help plan the trip enjoy the ride." As our children got older, Jeanne and I would always sit down with them prior to taking a vacation and involve them in the planning. So often, the anticipation was almost as enjoyable as the participation (well, not really, but it added to the enjoyment of the trip).

As I have shared, we involved associates in procedure changes by creating an ad hoc group. This allowed us to make the best decision by getting input from those mostly affected by the decision. And it allowed individuals to feel (and realize) that they were part of the decision. All too often, suggestions would pop up that leadership would have never thought of.

Likewise, we had the customer focus groups, from which we could get feedback on old programs and new alike. Not only would this allow consumers to critique our operation and give us a truer evaluation of how we were doing, but also it helped keep our team focused on our customer and why we set up the programs that we have.

Be intentional and consistent about *what* you communicate.

- Our motto to our customers was "From our family to yours," meaning we will never do less for you than we would do for our own family. You deserve our best.
- Our motto to our associates was "We are people working with people, serving people," meaning we were in the people business. Selling groceries was just the process in which we did it.
- Our quarterly associate publication *Off the Shelf* always portrayed our message and supported the wins of our associates.
- Many of our weekly advertisements, going out to over four hundred thousand homes, reflected statements of what we believed, enforcing our culture to our customers while at the same time to our associates (they read our advertising too!).

○ Throughout the year, in my little article on the front page, "Food for Thought," although mainly for helping people understand differences in food, and its history, etc., I would periodically feature articles like "Why we say our associates come first and our customers come second," "Why cleanliness is so important to Glen's Markets," "Why we value our customers," etc.

Picture of one of the last •Food for Thought• that was published on the front page of our 8-page advertisements. I used this to talk to our customer (and associates alike, as they too were customers)

- The entire front page of our CHRISTmas advertisement would feature the Baby Jesus and/or a current statement about what CHRISTmas means to us. (Again, I cannot spell CHRISTmas any differently because it is so important to me to not leave Christ out of CHRISTmas.)
- Likewise, the entire front page of our Easter advertisement would have the Cross with a statement of what Easter means. We weren't trying to push our beliefs on others, well maybe, but more so, that was who we were. More than once, I had a customer comment at they didn't share our "religious" beliefs but that to them, they got the message that we would strive to do everything fair and honest in trying to follow the "golden rule." (Do you know the words *golden rule* aren't even listed in the Bible?).

- Just like with our children, if we say one thing a hundred times but then say something different just once, they will latch on to that onetime exception. The importance of being consistent in what you say takes a lot of intentional ability. It must always be consistent.

Always make yourself available

I understand if you are a leader and responsible for the guidance of other people, your schedule is booked. We need to understand our associates' perspective. Trust me, if your team doesn't think you're available (whether you are or not), they will think one of three things: you are beyond approachable because of your superior attitude (may just be their perspective), you are just too busy for them to bother you, or they will think you really don't care or you would make yourself more available for them to share their questions, thoughts, and opinions.

To offer an "open-door" impression is really easier said than done. Although our offices were smaller when my dad was at the helm, he would walk around the offices almost every morning to just say "good morning." Did he do it every day? No, but he would do it more than just once or twice a week. Although he had never shared his intentionality of this, because of his example, I made it a habit to do the same thing. Was it harder with about eighty associates in the office? Probably, but there were groups working together (like the accounting office) that made it easier to just say, "Good morning. How's everyone doing this morning?" Every once in a while, I would throw in, "Is everyone still having fun?" That always brought a smile even though they probably had heard it a hundred times. I must have done the same thing when I visited stores as it wasn't uncommon for an associate to come up to me and say, "Hey, are we still having fun?"

Likewise, and an example from Dad, I would make it a point to visit each of our twenty-six stores at least every six to eight weeks, some because of their location, more often. The few in the Upper Peninsula of Michigan, an over three-hour drive, was more of a challenge, but I would coordinate those trips to ride with one of our departmental directors (meat director, produce director, etc.) or a district manager. This would also allow me time in a car to chat and *listen*.

In creating an atmosphere for associates to open up, except for those who directly worked with me, I would never critique anyone's work although I may point out something that may be helpful to them but never anything that they could take personal. As I walked a store, most often with the store manager or assistant store manager (if the manager was out, I rarely called that I was coming), I would seek to find something that someone was doing right, that is, the meat manager was working his case. If it were true, I might tell him how fresh his case looked and that I loved the variety he had out there. Or if the dairy manager was working his case, I might, if it was true, tell him that every time I'm in "his" store, his case always looks well stocked and ready for customers. If I saw something that wasn't right, normally, I wouldn't have to say anything as the manager I was walking with would notice it (to be addressed later after I left, so to not embarrass the department manager in front of me).

It's funny I developed such a habit of this that even today I may be in some city across these beautiful United States, in a grocery store, and see an awesome-looking produce or meat department (etc.). Jeanne gets a kick out of me because I will walk up to the person working the department, ask them if they are the manager (which they normally aren't), and tell them how great the department looks and what a great job they are doing. I think I have done that so many times to the associates in the fresh fish department at the Albertson's store in Livingston, Montana, that they probably recognize me.

As I had mentioned earlier, each of our associates were to wear their name tags (likewise, I always did too while visiting stores). Being able to call someone by their first name is a huge impact in opening up communications between individuals. Psychologists note that a person's name is the greatest connection to their own identity and individuality. Most concur that it is also the most important word in the world of that person (perhaps this reflects the self-centeredness that we are born with). As I did in our stores, I refer to waitresses, store clerks, and anyone who is wearing a name tag by their name. It is funny some of the looks on people's faces as they seemingly must forget they have a name tag on thus wonder for a moment how I know their name. True story, I called a man by his name (after seeing his name tag), and he then said, "Do I know you?" (we were fairly close to the same age), so I said, "We went to different schools together" (my humor). To which, he said, "I thought you looked familiar!" To which, I had to confess that I had seen his name tag.

When I was in my office, I never shut my door unless I had someone with me, and it was necessary that we were not interrupted. I have heard other leaders say they keep their door closed to help keep the noise down or so that they can have the privacy, but trust me, a closed door sends a signal, and it isn't "Welcome, I want to hear what is on your mind."

Always ask more questions than you give suggestions

Truly you have heard that saying that God has given us one mouth and two ears; hence, we should listen twice as much as we talk. Sadly, many leaders don't get this. If you wish to learn and understand what is really going on in your company or organization, shut up and listen!

First of all, no one likes to be told to do something even if you're the boss. Tell me one kid who enjoys their mom telling them to clean their room. Side story: Jeanne and I got tired of our two youngest children's rooms looking like, well, a teenager's room. My suggestion to Jeanne was telling them to clean them just wasn't doing it (and we had tried other things), so we told them the choice was theirs, it was their room: keep their room looking presentable or keep their door shut. Michelle's room took an astonishing makeover, and she left her door open. Travis, on the other hand, just kept his door closed. Was it the ideal solution? Not from Jeanne's perspective, but it allowed them to decide. Similarly, when I asked a store manager about the lack of cleanliness of the floors in his store and he shared that the night crew was behind and they hoped to get it in a couple of days, I would normally say, "Okay, but you need to schedule an associate at the front doors to let every customer know and understand why your floors do not look up to standards." And I would leave it that way. I seldom needed to do things like that, but almost 100% after I did, the next day the store manager would call me to just let me know the "situation" had been taken care of. The interesting part was the same challenge was never repeated. Were they told what to do? Well, kinda. But there was always an alternative left up to them. Again, almost always when the store manager called me, they would always add how much they appreciated how I had handled it.

When you ask a question about something and then just listen, it is surprising how much you often learn. The challenge in most cases is not to respond to anything bad from that conversation. Intentional leadership is long-term thinking and long-term leading. Like the story above, I have found much more results from asking questions about how a program or action is going and then just listening to the answer (or often excuses), but in some mysterious way, after those conversations, corrections seem to always take place much more rapidly. Having a conversation that isn't condemning, yet allowing the associate to come to the conclusion themselves that something isn't right (and he/she knows you know, but you're respecting his current status on it), will produce much more lasting results (it's like it sinks into a deeper level of the brain or something). But yet you are allowing the confidence and respect you have for that person not to be damaged. Trust me, most associates understand what you are doing with your questions, but respect the culture that you are trying to avoid embarrassment or your relationship with them from being damaged.

Are there times when you, as the leader, need to just give a more blunt direction? Certainly, but rarely, and with really rare occasions only with your immediate accountables and in private. I am sure there were times when I may have said, just plain and simple, "I would like to have it done!" but truly, I do not remember ever doing that. I do remember different times when I would say, "I really appreciate your thoughts on this, but I would really prefer to have it done this way." Would it be done? Sure. Just because someone has the authority, it doesn't mean you have to use it. The players know you and your position in the organization. The more they respect you, the more they will strive to get the results you both want.

With that, we need to often realize the power of the tongue. Proverbs 18:21 says, "The tongue has the power of life and death, and those who love it will eat its fruit." Hence, talk too much or say the wrong things, and you will, someday, be eating your words. Even more powerful than the tongue is the tone of the voice behind the words. Oh, this is so important when words are falling off the tongue of a leader, even if you are asking questions. Humans seem to make a lifetime from second-guessing what people are saying. Choice of words and tone of voice will always reflect your heart. A pastor friend of mine, Jim Mathis, has been quoted as saying, "The tongue brings the meaning of the heart out just as an anchor brings up what's on the bottom of the lake."

Lastly in listening, always strive to be in control of your eyes. Have you ever been talking to someone (or even when they are talking to you) and their eyes are roaming around the room or looking over your shoulder? Sure, you have. How did that make you feel? Were they really focusing on you and what you were saying? Of course not. Likewise, if you are talking to an associate and your eyes aren't fixed on their eyes or the jesters they are making with their hands, they are going to know you really aren't listening to them and that your interest in them is purely superficial. Make good eye contact with who you are listening to and who you are talking to. I have another pastor friend, Joe Sereno, who would always squat down when talking to small children, just to be able to make good eye contact, and give them his undivided attention. I have to admit I'm pretty good doing this with my grandchildren, but it probably ends there. I gotta work on that!

Always, always, always inspect what you expect!

The tag to the statement above is "don't let it be obvious that you are inspecting unless you see a major problem."

All companies have great programs, policies, and procedures, but the really great companies follow through and do them and do them right. Just because the managers you work with are good, that doesn't mean balls don't get dropped between the point of execution and the point of the customer experience. Having your eyes and ears open will allow you to ask the right questions to be assured that the business plan is working the way it should. All too often, I have asked someone about how a program is going, only for them to say, "I'm not sure, but with 'Pete' on it, I'm sure it's going well." Bottom line, without follow-through and inspecting what you expect, the chances are the results the customer is getting have been inappropriately changed by the various "Pete's" perspective, understanding, commitment, or who knows what. *Inspect what you expect.*

When you inspect what you expect, you not only support your team in getting better and the results for the customer to become better, but your team is empowered to carry out the "plan" for results. Without you saying it, they know what you are doing and will respect your management style of not meddling in their responsibility yet taking an interest to keep them strong and on track. All these are great cultural elements that build respect and trust.

Celebrate the wins and communicate the
loses, but don't dwell on the loses

Scream about the successes in your organization. We did that through cards and letters to our associates, announcements in our quarterly newsletter *Off the Shelf*, and through our annual stakeholder's meeting where in the presence of 1,200–1,500 people, multiple awards would be handed out. I think the different stores would see who could cheer the loudest for those from their store receiving something, and that wasn't all that bad, and it was something that they always shared that they had never experienced in any other "job." If people are important to your organization, use every element to let that come across loud and clear.

However, people screw up, and they make mistakes. We all do. Dishonesty was totally not tolerated at Glen's, that was a known factor, but most other infractions we accepted as people just being people. Would they be reprimanded? Based on the situation, certainly. But it was not the business of other associates in their store to know (although I know and you know that people do find out, but it should never be through leadership). I heard my dad tell me many times making a mistake is not necessarily a bad thing as long as you learn from it and do not make the same mistake again. Boy, I think I invented new mistakes because I sure made a lot of them!

In meetings, always expose the elephant in the room

We all know that there are things we don't talk about in meetings. Really? If everything is not exposed, do you really expect to make the best decision possible for the organization? If you are not aware of elephants in the room, they are situations in an organization that everyone knows but no one wants to talk about. And because no one wants to talk about them, decisions are made in spite of them, leading to less than effective decisions.

The best statement I had heard, and I used it every time when I lead a meeting focused on making decisions, was "What is said here, stays here, when we leave here." Hence, we need to put everything on the table so that we can make the best decisions, but if there is something that is not anyone else's business, then it should not be talked about outside this meeting. That includes if there is something that I have been doing to hinder things. Some of my most valuable team have shared privately with me, things that I have done that were hindering the process (and I valued their honesty and boldness for it). I love these honest people. In return, I had no respect or interest in having butt kissing bureaucrats on our team. We did have them, but if they didn't change, I would make a change.

Leaders, focus on what only you can do

If you desire to grow your organization, delegating actions that others can do is extremely important. There is so much that only you can do. No one else can do it. If you don't do it because you are doing something that someone else could be doing, then it is not going to get done. What? I only have so much I can do in meetings, in my office, or with the connections that I have to make. What do I do with my time? Let me reverse the question: What kind of an impact on the culture can you, as the leader, make just by your presence (no words even necessary) that no one else can make?

Surely, I could have kept my crazy hours busy doing other things than visiting stores on a regular basis, but the impact on our culture was priceless. If I walked into a store and they were busy at the front end, I loved to jump in and bag groceries, talk to customers, and be alongside cashiers and baggers. I know many times they wondered who was this guy off the street that started bagging groceries and asking customers how their day was going. But I know after I had walked just out of earshot, they would know. I cannot imagine it was ever a negative thing. I also knew it was a good example for the store leadership and others from our offices when they visited stores. Take care of the customer, and never forget that *every job* is important!

When at all possible, have an assistant that can "handle the little stuff." Just never confuse "people" with little stuff, and also realize there really isn't any "little stuff."

Plus by delegating things that others could be doing, you are also showing confidence in those you hand off projects to. But it is still important to "inspect what you expect."

Encourage everyone in leadership to spend time with the customers

Whether it is a meat director in front of a meat case asking customers how they are doing and if there were anything that they would like that they haven't experienced or a church staff person periodically acting as a greeter at the doors. People who are making decisions in an organization need to make contact with the final product, the customer, to help keep the pulse of why we are doing what we are doing and if we are doing it right. Again, eyes and ears open and complete eye contact.

Although I would rarely get negative feedback when stopping a customer to ask how we were doing, I knew it would open a door with that customer so that if she did have something that she wished to share, she would do it before she would walk out the door and then go somewhere else because she might be unhappy about something. Of course, the standard comment I would often get would be "It would be nice if you lowered your pricing," almost always followed by a smile. Everyone wants lower prices. I wouldn't just smile and walk away. Even if it were a passing comment, it did give me an opportunity to talk to one of our customers (between my name tag and my picture being on the front page of our advertising for the "Food for Thought" article, they always seem to know who I was). To that comment, I would always share that we work hard to bring the variety of products and the service they should expect at the best competitive pricing. I was sure some of our competition may be less expensive on somethings, and likewise, we would be priced lower on some than they. It was something that we worked hard on. Whether they believed me or not, I believe they understood I was trying to being honest with them.

If you build cars, but never drive one. How in the world do you know if you are building them right? Or better yet, the way the consumer desires it?

Know that you do not know everything; thus, seek counsel

Of course, if you are going into court, you would seek the best attorney to help you with the legalities. But who really knows all there is to know about the business you are in? If you think you do, without even knowing you, I can tell you that you are wrong!

I do not remember what position I was in our family company, I may have still been stocking shelves and bagging groceries when I walked into my dad's office, and he was on the phone. When he got off the phone, he shared that he was talking to an individual at Spartan Stores who he had a lot of confidence in. "You know one of the greatest tools I have is this telephone?" he said. This would have been in the mid to late 1960s, so email, Google, computers, texting, and the like were not heard of yet. Getting on a commercial airplane to travel somewhere was unheard of, and certainly not many people were traveling that way. "With this phone," he continued, "I can bounce ideas off almost anyone to get their opinion. Of course, after I get their opinion, it is still my responsibility to make the right decision."

Over the years, we had hired consultants in different areas: marketing, customer satisfaction, associate relationship, etc. Most were extremely helpful, some may not have been so, but we always became better because of it.

We encouraged our leaders to see what our competition was doing and see what other operators in the country were doing. It wasn't our intent to be on the cutting edge all the time, but it was important that if we desired to take care of our associates, serve our customers, and satisfy our stockholders, we needed to be in the know and at least aware of where the cutting edge was.

From looking through my glasses, the leader who thinks they know it all and thus does not need to seek outside help is like the guy who doesn't go to a doctor until they are really sick. That individual, when they do finally go to a doctor, most often finds it too late. Such is the leader who thinks he knows it all.

When others are striving to accomplish the same result that you are, why would you always want to try and reinvent the wheel?

Our team would read about and sometimes traveled to other grocery groups to help understand areas where we could make Glen's a better place for our associates and our customers.

Leadership involves community involvement

This may or may not seem a little odd, but each of our locations were located in smaller communities (although mostly county seats). Our communities ranged from 2,500 to 13,000 in population although our customer base came from the entire county and often neighboring counties.

We encouraged our leadership to be community minded and to enjoy some kind of community involvement. The chamber of commerce (which many of our store managers, like myself, served on chamber boards and even terms as president), service clubs (Rotary Club, Lions Club, etc.), local school programs and/or sports, and local festival boards, the options were numerous. Why might you say? Is there some place that you shop because you know the people there? Sure, there is, especially in a smaller community. Also, our leadership was good at what they did; hence, they would have been extremely beneficial to any organization.

Having leadership involved in your community adds a human, personal face to your business or organization. It also allows leadership to hear local comments (good or helpful) about your organization; things that you may have never had the opportunity to hear from a customer that could be vital to the success of your business.

This also "drags" your organization into the community. If your leadership is involved, he/she is going to get your organization involved. One blends into the other for the benefit of both. It also helps leadership maintain a pulse of the communities that we were serving.

My brother-in-law and partner, Denny, was a basketball freak. The Gus Macker organization came to us about becoming a key sponsor in having an annual 3-on-3 Gus Macker tournament in Gaylord. The sponsorship for them to come to town was $10,000. It's a lot of money now, but even more so in the early 1990s. Denny, especially, had been involved in the local sports program. Although we had never pledged that much funds for anything other than local hospitals or schools, we made the commitment. The result was over three hundred four-kid/man teams signed up the first year, bringing their parents and families to Gaylord for a weekend (can you multiply that in your head; that's 1,200 players plus family and friends the first year. It was huge!), and it continued to grow to over one thousand teams until the organization had to limit the sign-up because of lack of space and volunteers. Meanwhile, all those basketball courts sported the Glen's Market logo along with the thousands of T-shirts that every player wore. Around northern Michigan, years later, I would still see those T-shirts being worn. It was good for the community, and it was good for our business too.

To this day, the Glen's logo is still on basketball and football scoreboards around the northern part of Michigan, all because Glen's Markets' leadership got involved.

You may say, "Well, our organization isn't in a small community. How do we make an impact in our area?" That's the key—in your area, in your marketing area. There are still schools, organizational clubs, etc. Making your "brand" known is good business, but it is also rewarding for your team and their value of being part of something bigger than themselves.

A side note, which is really more important, our communities need the involvement and support from the businesses and organizations within them. We were quick to support our hospitals, our school events, the kids in the Future Farmers of America Programs, the sports program, etc. If you desire your organization to be part of the community, you need to have your team (and your dollars) be part of the community. It is not a one-way street. In 1985, my dad put together a trust that from its investment growth pays for every fourth grader in each of the schools in Otsego County (Gaylord Community Schools, Vanderbilt School, Johannesburg/Lewiston Schools, St. Mary's Catholic School, and the Otsego Christian School) to have eight swimming lessons. Each of the schools, early on, bought into the program by scheduling accordingly and busing the children to and from the Gaylord Sportsplex. This was something that he felt was important for every child to learn. That was over thirty-five years ago, and as I write this, one of our granddaughters and one of our grandsons are going through the swimming lessons right now. One hundred percent covered by a trust Dad set up to help give back to his community.

Way back in the beginning, Dad got us involved
in our communities (he personally help build
this float for the Gaylord Alpenfest

Denny with one of the Glen's created Alpenfest mascots

The importance of a good accountant

Unless you are a "bean counter," this may seem like a little different topic to touch on when talking about intentional leadership, being frank—all a business is, is the process or a gamble that more dollars come in through the cash registers then go out in paying bills.

Whether your organization is large enough to have your own chief financial officer (CFO) or you use a software program like QuickBooks and then pass the information onto an accountant at the end of the year, the right person in the final decision-making position of your finances has a huge impact on how much funds will be retained after paying Uncle Sam (and whoever is your state governor).

Early on, my dad's older brother, Uncle Keith, joined our company after retiring from a career with the US Navy. The expertise that he had learned in his position with the Navy became a huge asset to us. When Keith retired, we were fortunate to obtain the accountant that Keith worked with in the accounting offices at Spartan Stores Inc.

Eric Buckleitner was more than an accountant. He understood finance, and he didn't hesitate to ask someone more experienced or knowledgeable than he if he had a question. Eric taught me the importance of cash flow over the bottom line on a profit/loss statement. Eric would never consider "cooking-the-books." Instead, like Uncle Keith, he pursued best accounting practices that allowed us to stay within the confines of the law (the IRS) and yet allowed us to defer paying any more taxes than we legally needed to. I chuckle when I think of the combination of his extreme conservativeness and my eternal-optimist thinking. We actually blended very well. As with so many of our team that I have not been able to mention in this writing, he was an invaluable asset to Glen's Markets. I continue to value his friendship too.

Do not underestimate the impact of a talented individual overseeing your finances.

Robert Keith Catt (1923–2018) helped his brother
by skillfully guiding all accounting matters

Eric Bucklietner, our V.P. Finance & Accounting,
was to me what Keith was to my Dad

Know the difference between responsibility and accountability

Lastly, there is a *huge* difference between responsibility and accountability. Oh, so often, I have gotten into a debate that the two words mean the same. Do not fall to that deception.

When you are a leader of people, you train, direct, and then give up responsibility to them. *But* you are still always accountable. Let me say that again. You never give up accountability! No matter what level of leadership you are performing, perhaps someone else has given you responsibility over a division, department, etc. You probably have other people you work with in that area. To empower them, you give them responsibility (and don't take it away), but nevertheless, you never give up the accountability. Hence, that is why you have to continually inspect what you expect.

I learned this the hard way. One of my very best friends, and a strong Christian mentor to me, was one whom I had the most confidence in, probably anyone I have ever worked with. We worked extremely close and directly together. Because of my confidence, I gave him the most responsibility of anyone else in our company; however, I also didn't question any of the directions he desired to go with those responsibilities. I later realized that I had not only relinquished my responsibilities, but I also relinquished *my* own accountabilities to him. You might say I gave him a free hand and didn't inspect what I expected of the directions he was taking us. (Now, let me be very clear. The direction he was going could have been extremely successful in another company. He was [and is] a good man.) However, it was different from what we had been doing and the direction that I felt we needed to head. By the time I realized it and we had the needed conversation, "that conversation," his confidence had, understandably, grown to where he challenged my thoughts. (One of the things I always enjoyed and appreciated was I never had to second-guess him. He was always honest.) Although I always enjoyed my thoughts challenged, deciding where walking paths are going as compared to main highways are much different. This ended up bringing us to an in passing that resulted in us having to decide to head different ways. Although I still consider him to be a great and faithful friend, I know it is not the same. However, I still have a great love and respect for him.

I am reminded of another story that took a different turn. We had an opportunity to purchase a very successful drugstore. We had pharmacies in some of our stores; thus, we felt if nothing else, one day we could incorporate the pharmacy business of the drugstore into our store that was in the same center. Upon closing the sale, I asked the owner, who was also a good acquaintance, why he would wish to sell his store that was doing so well and yet he wasn't ready to retire. His answer still echoes in my mind: "I love what I'm doing. I have always loved the business." He continued, "But after—joined me, I was extremely pleased with him, so I allowed him to purchase 10 percent of my business. Now, years later, I just can't work with him anymore. And I just cannot bring myself to confront him." And he gave reasons that had nothing to do with honesty or production. Because his business was so successful, I offered him an out for him not to sell. He could afford to pay his 10 percent partner a premium to buy out the 10 percent, but again, he said he just would not be able to confront the individual with the truth. I felt so sorry for my friend as he preferred to sell his lifetime business rather than take the accountability of a decision that needed to be done.

So often…oh, so often, we learn the most from our mistakes. I have seen my experience with my dear friend repeated most often in different companies and organizations. Communications, feedback, and inspecting what you expect are all so true even with your most trusted and respected comrades. If you value them, you will work hard to empower them but also stay close to them and take the final accountability that is yours, only yours.

Building a positive, self-creating culture is a full-time awareness

All that I have talked about in this book is what we practiced at Glen's Markets and what we preached to our associates. Many of our peers in our industry have shared their admiration about our culture. Each time we would hire a consultant, after spending time in our offices and around our stores, the comment would always be the same: "It is rare, if ever, that I have experienced the spirit and cama-raderie across the board in associates as I have witnessed at Glen's Markets." We had one individual who was nationally known within the retail grocery industry and one that I would personally work with when he would visit. After three years, I shared how valuable he had been to us (and especially me as a new president of the business), but it was time to make a break. He shared that he really wanted to continue as he felt although he knew marketing, he had been getting an education in relational leadership. He said he had marveled about our culture from his first visit.

Building a strong, self-creating culture *takes full-time awareness*. It is probably the most intentional thing a leader can do. And it starts with being an example. Everything you say or perhaps don't say makes a statement. Everything you do or don't do makes a statement. So it goes with each individual who works directly with you, and so it goes with each associate who has contact with your customers.

Nobody operates a business or organization better than the owner. The closest element is when associates feel empowered to make decisions and act as if the business is theirs.

CHAPTER 7

Why Did We Decide to Sell Glen's Markets?

How blessed is the man who finds wisdom and the man who gains understanding. For her profit is better than the profit of silver and her gain better than fine gold. She is more precious than jewels; and nothing you desire compares with her.

—Proverbs 3:13

When someone decides to sell something, whether it be a business, a home, a boat, or a jar of homemade jam, there is a reason. Some reasons are simple and self-explanatory, while other reasons seem much more complex. Of course, there is always the "want to," "have to," or "just seems like the right thing to do" reasons.

Making the decision to sell a business that has been in the family for forty-eight years, and going into its third generation, doesn't just happen overnight. (It's funny, but numerous people have asked me why we didn't wait for our fiftieth anniversary to sell. Not sure what that would have to do with such a major decision, but it was always interesting to reflect on the different individuals who asked such a question.)

I think if I had a $10 bill for each one of our friends, past associates, or past customers who have told me that they wished that we had not sold, I think we could have bought the company back. I have always taken those comments as a compliment. Our associates were exceptional. "Nobody does (did) it better!" The culture created by happy and committed associates is priceless in a business atmosphere.

As I reflect back, there are actually five different reasons that entered into the decision to sell Glen's Markets. Perhaps the first, my father coming into my office, and the second, Glen B coming into my office, were the key elements, but the others were each strong considerations.

Reason 1

It was the summer of 1995. Dad was back in Gaylord for his annual four-month stay from sunny Florida, his main residence for the last number of years. In between his golf games, he would periodically stop by the offices for a cup of coffee. When Dad came to the offices, although it had been well over ten years since he had been around (kind of) full-time, he was still like a celebrity. He would still walk through the offices shaking hands and kissing babies (as the saying goes) with each of our eighty-plus office associates. Some of them are new since his departure (although they knew of his legend), but still the majority of those he had worked with were still around.

He would always come down to my office if I were there, located at the end of the outside wall of the offices. I would normally be his last stop. As much as I enjoy chatting with my dad, in my mind, he was still kind of a celebrity to me too. I always had a high admiration and respect for him. It always seemed like after about fifteen minutes, he would say, "I know you're busy, and I don't want to take up much of your time...yada yada yada," and he would be out the door. In the past, he had had good friends stop by his office and seem to chat for an hour or longer. Nevertheless, I always valued the time with him.

This particular morning when Dad stopped by, he chose to stay a little longer. He definitely had something on his mind. He actually shut the door behind him, something that he had never done. Our offices always had an open-door policy, but if someone's door was shut, well, you just waited until it was open again.

He knew something that he had not shared with the rest of the family yet, including me. And this morning, he still wasn't going to share it either, but I later figured it was the basic motivation for his "little talk."

He had recently found out that he had "another" aneurysm. His first aneurysm was mistakenly discovered in 1985 when he had gone for a checkup on a quad bypass heart surgery that he had a couple of years before. At that time, evidently, the x-ray technician had positioned their equipment a little lower than needed to view the current condition of the repairs made to his heart. In evaluating the results, his doctor noticed a bulge on his main artery, right where it forked going to each of his legs. A month later, he returned from a medical center in Milwaukee with a small pair-of-pants-looking device stitched around the forking of that major artery intended to prevent any further occurrence of having a fatal problem. Obviously, we were all grateful for the error that the technician had made. Likewise, Dad, knowing that aneurysms are caused mainly by stress, started making adjustments in how he handled challenges in life. We were also aware that aneurysms are hereditary as my grandfather, his dad (Pop), had passed seven years earlier from an aneurysm bursting. Discovering aneurysms before they become deadly is still rare today.

This aneurysm was located on the artery located on the back side of his heart. Once he finally shared his situation with us (months later), he said that the doctor said even though sixty-nine years of age, he was a good candidate for a heart transplant, which would have been the only option to take care of this kind of situation. However, Dad said that he had chosen not to go with that option as he felt he had already had enough "hospital time." His comment was that he had had a great life, he knew where he was going, and knowing the aneurysm could burst at any time, it could also hold off for a number of years. His standard comment was, "Had I known I was going to live this long, I would have taken better care of my body." And then he would laugh. Seriously, his biggest concern was the ten minutes between the burst and when life (in that body) would be over. Although we dearly miss him, God truly blessed him when the time came on March 30 the following year. The aneurysm started leaking at some point during the night, and the following morning, Dad's body just didn't wake up. During the night, his spirit was taken away to be with his Lord.

This August morning in '95, when he stopped by, after the general *how are things going?* Dad got serious about some of his feelings. "So you and Denny should think about selling the company at some time." Wow, I will never forget those words coming out of his mouth. I think you could have knocked me off my chair with a feather. However, at the time, I didn't let it sink in.

In spite of numerous times we had been contacted by larger companies wishing to purchase Glen's Markets, my pad answer has always been that we had absolutely no interest in discussing it.

"What?" was my reply. "We would never consider selling the company!" Truly, we had never even entertained the notion. I couldn't even believe those words had come out of his mouth.

Dad carried on his conversation about knowing the hours that he worked and that we work, the stress on our bodies, and the lack of time we have available to spend with our families, the ones we love the most. He reminisced that if he could have a do-over, he would have just kept one store or perhaps had stopped with three stores. He said he's thought about it, and he could have spent more time with "us kids," and we still would have had much of the financial flexibility. With Dad, the business was never about the money or how much he could make. It was always about creating financial security for the family and opportunities for each of those working with him—the result of growing up during the Great Depression where his dad was unemployed and they worked and lived day to day and mouth to mouth.

I, as well as I'm sure my siblings, had never had any thoughts that our dad was ignoring us because of the business. We grew up in a family business, and we seemed to understand the natural sacrifices that came with that (although we didn't think of them as sacrifices at the time). Sure, we saw other dads doing different things with their families, but at least for me, I never once ever thought I had been short-sided. I shared that with Dad and thanked him for providing a living and a working future for us. The values that he had installed with us, at least to me, was beyond the family vacations and some of the experiences that I had seen some of my other friends enjoy with their dads. Every family experiences their own experiences. From those experiences, you either become bitter or better. As for our family, most of us were much better because of our experiences.

When Dad left the office that morning, I surmise he carried the same baggage with him as he did when he came in. As for me, my thoughts had been jarred somewhat. At the time, all his words hadn't really sunk in too deep though I think my thoughts had been more directed toward the regrets that I suspected he was going through. Little did I know that a paradigm shift, probably caused by his health condition, was probably causing a paradigm shift to start taking hold of my thinking. Months later when he announced his health situation, the pieces started to come together, but I still don't think I ever shared his "selling" thoughts, not even to Denny, and I never kept anything from him.

Other factors in selling

After the unknowingly opening of my brain by Dad's comments, other elements started to take place a couple of years later. I am listing these in no particular order.

During those couple of years, Denny Freeman, my partner (along with Sandy) in buying my father out, decided to retire from the company and become a full-time pastor. Although he kept his position of executive VP, and his office which he continued to work from, the majority of his accountabilities were turned over to others in the department. Denny's presence had left an immeasurable impression on our associates and how we handled them. Although I did feel comfortable with those we selected to cover his areas, his heart would always be irreplaceable.

The interest in purchasing our company continued to only intensify. The economy was as strong as it had ever been. Big companies were getting bigger and looking for ways to expand. Glen's Markets were located in twenty-three different communities, and in virtually every one of them, we were fortunate to be the market leader. Generating over $265 million a year in sales across northern Michigan and the eastern side of the Upper Peninsula, our company offered a large market share for an outsider to be able to move in and start getting their foothold in the Michigan market. We knew all this, but prior to Dad's conversation with me three years prior, those factors never seemed to hold water. In my mind, Glen's was going to be a family company for generations to come. Dad started it. I had two sons interested in working the business, Glen B. and Travis, and Glen now had a young son, Tanner Glen, who could very possibly be the fourth generation.

Another reason

With the intensity of the Kroger, the A&P, and SuperValu having third parties contact us to test the waters, my son Glen B. stopped by to have a serious conversation with me.

Glen had started as a stocker and bagger in our Kalkaska store when he was fourteen years old. After high school and a short stint in college, he came into the company full-time. Over the next fifteen years, Glen worked in seven different stores, each time moving to a new store and community when he received a well-earned promotion. Opening the Oscoda store was his first experience as the store manager himself, which proved successful from his past experience. He had an opportunity to do a one-year internship at Spartan Stores, our main supplier, giving him a brief but overall experience at wholesale, including being given the marketing savvy of opening Spartan's first downtown Detroit store.

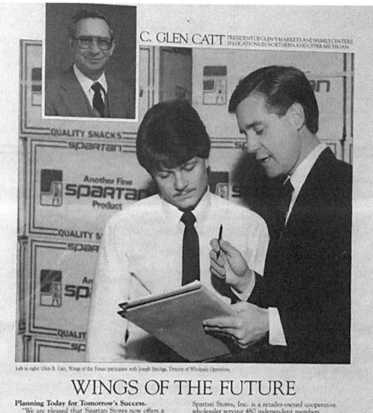

WINGS OF THE FUTURE

Planning Today for Tomorrow's Success.

"We are pleased that Spartan Stores now offers a program to help member retailers prepare our succession for a smooth transition of ownership and management. Forty-one of Glen's associates are currently enrolled in Wings of the Future. The program provides an excellent opportunity to gain knowledge and experience outside our store environment. We feel the program will be extremely valuable to the future of our business."

Wings of the Future provides family business successors — sons, daughters and entrusted others — with a practical and realistic perspective on business continuity. The ten month program consists of a series of workshops, seminars, warehouse visits, summer work programs and training sessions. Participants are taken "under our wing" at Spartan to help them better understand the basic management concepts essential to the successful growth and perpetuation of a family-owned business.

Spartan Stores, Inc. is a retailer-owned cooperative wholesaler serving 480 independent members throughout Michigan, Indiana and Ohio.

Join successful Spartan retail customers like C. Glen Catt who have invested their future with Spartan Stores.
For more information, call 616-878-2284 or write Market Development, Spartan Stores, Inc., P.O. Box 8700, Grand Rapids, MI 49518.

Circle No. 13 on Reader Service Card

Glen B Catt during his 1-year of Spartan Wholesale training

Later, we decided to open our own warehouse distribution center, and we purchased a small fleet of semi-tractor trucks. This was a new venture for us, but Glen B. seemed to know the right questions to ask and the right people to ask them to. A 50,000-square-foot location that would allow our purchasing power to buy direct on large-volume items and deliver them to our retail stores, along with purchasing eight semi-tractors and seventeen large trailers, allowed us to also start picking up our dry grocery merchandise from Spartan Stores downstate and deliver them to our stores. We analyzed that not only could we save $.23 per mile in delivery costs, but we also had more accuracy as to the timing when the trucks would be at the stores, allowing for better scheduling at store level. (This operation also became priceless in allowing us to pick up the President's Choice line of merchandise as I had mentioned earlier.)

The warehouse and trucking direction were totally new to us, but it was something that we placed in Glen's hands, and he was able to organize and execute in an exceptional way.

One of our road signs that traveled across Michigan daily

Later, Glen transferred directly into the general offices, overseeing the day-to-day operation of our retail, wholesale, and trucking operations.

So back to Glen coming into my office, Glen started the conversation with "I've been thinking" (which always scares a Dad with an aggressive son in the business, ha ha). He continued relaying his thoughts of all the hours that he had seen and heard his grandpa had worked, the hours that he had witnessed that I had put in over the years, and the commitment of hours that he had been working. He said he didn't mind the hours, and he would be good with it for another ten to fifteen years or so. But being in his early thirties, it wasn't something that he really wanted to be doing for another twenty-five to thirty years. Hence, maybe we should test the waters on selling the company. Hm, I had never shared my dad's conversation from three years earlier. In fact, as I had mentioned, I had never shared it with my sister or Denny or anyone. But now, Dad's conversation started coming back to me, almost like a haunting.

Yet another reason

Walmart had been opening their Super Walmart locations in northern Michigan with more being considered. Although we viewed Walmart with groceries as a large "price" competitor, we were confident that the quality of our perishable departments, meat, produce, deli, and bakery, along with the culture of our associates and the service that they offered, could hold our position on any perceived price disadvantage that we might have. We were ready to buckle down to defend our marketing areas.

However, along with the competitive Walmart threat, having friends in the Meijer Headquarters, in Grand Rapids, we were aware that they too had other areas in northern Michigan that they were looking at putting their super, 200,000-square-foot stores, and we had heard that Gaylord, Petoskey, and Alpena were rumored to each have one of them. We had stores in each of those locations; however, with the additional marketing area of a Meijer, we knew the effect of just those three stores would affect the sales in at least eleven of our stores. (Years prior, Meijer was also a Spartan retailer. Their interest in getting more involved in dry goods, and [at the time] Spartan's lack of interest in supplying that product, drove Meijer toward becoming their own owner/operator wholesaler.) At Glen's, we had always had a great respect for how the Meijer family operated, much like the floor plan we had put together that had led to the success of Glen's Markets in smaller markets. With the Meijer group looking at moving to northern Michigan, and knowing the reaching effect on so many of our locations, forced us to look at them as a much more serious threat. Could our company survive? We were sure we could. Would it be stressful and eat up our profits for a number of years? Without a doubt, it no doubt would.

As I mentioned, during this whole time, the economy was great, and we were continually being pursued by other companies asking if we would be interested in coming to the table to talk about selling. The economy at Glen's Markets was great too. Our sales had continued to grow at a double-digit percentage. A number of our long-term decisions that we had been making over the years were now paying off, and our profits had been continually running above the industry average.

Along with the many companies and individuals whom we consulted with, a practice Dad had always shared was priceless, reminding us that it was always important to seek out the best consultants you could find; however, we still had to be accountable for the final decision. A gentleman whom we had relied on heavily for a number of years for financial input and direction was Gary Milligan. Gary was a partner with Crowe Chizek, an accounting conglomerate that to this day has continued to grow to become our country's seventh largest accounting network. Gary had known of the interests in Glen's Markets, but his respect on how we operated always seemed to be an encouragement for us to keep looking straight ahead. Although he wasn't a retailer, Gary knew the financial territory of our business as well as we did (perhaps better). He had been involved in every aspect of our financials for over a dozen years: accounting, investments, financing, tax planning, corporate development, and estate planning.

Gary was a great educator, and he helped us to understand that any possible financial transaction in selling a company of our size would involve the transaction price to be based on its EBITDA (the *e*arnings *b*efore *i*nterest, *t*axes, *d*epreciation, and *a*mortization). Hence, the financial stability and cash flow of the company would determine the negotiating of the sale of the company. For the "bean counters" of pursuing companies, this would be the key factor that they would be looking at and consulting accordingly.

After getting what we considered our "Family Executive Team" together, Denny, Eric Buckleitner (our chief financial officer [CFO]), Glen B., and myself, along with Gary, we considered the elements and decided to "go fishing." To go fishing means let's test the water, but we still knew that we were in control of what fish we would keep, if any. No decision would need to be made until we started the motor to head back to shore. Just because we were going to open discussions with potential buyers didn't mean we would have to pull the trigger if we didn't want to. We didn't have to sell, we didn't necessarily want to sell, it was just that the atmosphere for fishing right now looked pretty exceptional, and the future of filling the pantry with continued strong success in the future was questionable. Nevertheless, Gary gave us a detailed, financial target of what he thought we would get for the retail part of the company (including our trucking and small warehouse operation, but not to include our commercial real estate operation that owned half the properties that housed our supermarkets, along with small shopping centers attached to them). With that, Gary also offered his opinion of a top target that he thought we could focus on, a target which he felt would offer an interest of return where we may wish to pull the trigger.

Along with working with Crowe, Gary connected us with KPMG. At the time, KPMG was one of the largest in their industry as a global network that offered audit and tax advisory services. Their expertise in marketing businesses was out of our realm of thinking. Obviously, for Gary, he never had any sides to boxes that he worked in; his thinking was always outside the box.

Our team met with Gary and the KPMG team, and they put together a strategy to market Glen's Markets. The process ended up taking almost two years. In the end, we had seven different companies in the bidding process, not a sealed bidding but an open book, negotiating type of bidding. Kroger, A&P, Minnesota-based SuperValu, Michigan-based Spartan Stores, Wisconsin-based Roundy's, Mississippi-based Jitney-Jungle Stores, and an out-of-state group of investors, whom from what I could find out (they were quite secretive), had never had experience in operating supermarkets. Each of our pursuers were mid and eastern US based, but only Spartan Stores was Michigan based. We had heard that there was an overseas company that inquired, but it ended up they felt our locations would not have been conducive for them.

Spartan Stores was probably our number one choice, at the time, to purchase our company. We had worked closely with them since the second year Dad gave birth to his company. Dad had spent twenty-five years on their board of directors (one term as the president, just prior to him guiding the board to name a full-time working president), and I had spent ten years on the Spartan board of directors, abstaining from attending meetings the last year because of the conflict of interest in the negotiating process.

As the negotiations continued, the first to drop out were the Jitney-Jungle and the wild card investors. I am sure for Jitney-Jungle, with all their stores in mid-south of the country, they would have only had interest in a steal of a deal. Likewise, I suspect for the investment group. Obviously, their interest would be to pick up a company at a great value, operate them for a while, and then spin them off for a larger return.

The challenge with our company for other retailers and for investment companies was, financially, there was little room for improvement. Their type of company did not have the synergies from which they could springboard into further growth as compared to out-of-state wholesalers who could view the project as suddenly picking up a large Michigan market share and hence would have been the interest for the likes of Kroger, A&P, SuperValu, and Roundy's. For Spartan Stores, just the opposite was their motivation. They stood to lose their second largest customer, purchasing over $100 million a year, along with opening the Michigan market to a new, large, outside competitor.

When all was said and done, Spartan Stores became the winning survivor in the bidding process and purchased the supermarket operations of our company. The current economy, the financial strength of our company (thanks to our team), and the strategic bidding process (thanks to Crowe Chizek and KPMG) resulted in bringing a

33% higher sale price than our financial friend Gary had targeted as the top price to go for. Unquestionably, if you are fishing for big fish, and you bring in a record size catch, you take it home and we did. The only thing left was to negotiate leases on the buildings that we owned, which we were able to get twenty-year leases on three of them and fifteen-year leases on the others, all with numerous five-year options. This left three Save-A-Lot stores (limited assortment operations) and our laundry and dry cleaning operation. Denny's three sons, Tim, Tom, and Paul, purchased those businesses, forming their own operation, since then they have grown their number of Save-A-Lots considerably and sold the laundry and dry cleaners (which we still lease to the new owners).

The above makes it seem like it was an easy decision to make. Well, let me tell you, it wasn't. It certainly wasn't! The psychological stress of making that kind of move on such a large "material" object that had been in the family for so many years was mind boggling.

But there was one more element that had prepared me for this move.

About a year prior to all the above transaction, I had done a personal Bible study on the book of Ecclesiastes, a book in the Bible authored by King Solomon through the spiritual direction of our Creator. Solomon, one of the sons of King David, was considered not only one of the richest individuals who have ever walked the earth but more so the one who had been given the most wisdom. He was wise beyond his years when he answered God's question to him. In 1 Kings, the story reads:

> In Gibeon [a city just north of Jerusalem] the Lord appeared to Solomon in a dream at night; and God said, "Ask whatever you wish Me to give you."

Wow, can you imagine God, the creator of the universe, everything that our eyes can see and our ears can hear and of anything that we will ever experience, would say to you, "Ask whatever you wish me to give to you"? Would not most of us say *buku* of dollars, or something about our health or a loved one's health, or for a long life? But what does it say Solomon said:

> Then Solomon said, "You have shown great lovingkindness to Your servant David my father, according as he walked before You in truth and righteousness and uprightness of heart towards You; and You have reserved for him this great lovingkindness, that You have given him a son to sit on his throne, as it is this day. Now, O Lord my God, You have made Your servant king in place of my father David, yet I am but a little child; I do not know how to go out or come in. [Solomon was only twelve years old when he became the king, following his father. However, he was already married and had a one-year-old son at this time, Rehoboam. However, marrying that young was not uncommon at that time.] Your servant is in the midst of Your people which You have chosen, a great people who are too many to be numbered or counted. So [and this is Solomon's answer to God's question. Don't miss it!] give Your servant an understanding heart to judge Your people to discern between good and evil. For who is able to judge this great people of Yours?" (1 Kings 3:6-9)

Of all the things Solomon could have asked for from God, he asked for wisdom. Picturing myself in that kind of situation, I really wondered what I would have asked for. I pondered on that for quite a while. It actually resulted in my asking for wisdom every morning, not God's wisdom because I knew something like that, even if He were to grant it, was not something that I would be able to handle but for wisdom for whatever I may face that day.

History credits King Solomon with authoring the book of Ecclesiastes, the book of *Songs of Songs*, and most of the book of Proverbs. Solomon had written these books late in his life (somewhere around 935 BC), after he had experienced a lifetime of living with exceptional wisdom. Literally, he had become a product of the mistakes he had made throughout his life, and through his gained wisdom, he began to document them.

As I read about Solomon living with this exceptional wisdom, I could see he portrayed the results of his success and blessings, the challenges those brought, and then his lifelong evaluation of what was really important after having everything. It caused me to ponder on my own life.

Surely, I didn't acquire the wisdom that Solomon had, nor did I have unlimited funds or the opportunity to do whatever I wished with this life. Life was good, but I had already realized that where I was placing my roughly 120-awake hours that are in a week wasn't lining up with what was really important to me. Nevertheless, at the time, I do not think I really made any changes, but little did I know, this starting-of-a-shift-in-thinking was going to play a huge part in future decisions that I would be faced with.

There are basically four takes from the Solomon's writings: human yearning, moral values, our fallen nature, and ultimate accountability.

Human yearning

Solomon bears witness to a fundamental restlessness in the human spirit. Man is never satisfied. Oh, does this sound familiar? We yearn for ambition, fame, wealth, pleasure, and to know the future. Most of these traits hit home for me as I read them. I was looking to fill my ambitions, to please my father, always interested in personal pleasure, and looking to the future wondering what it may bring. I drove myself and our team at Glen's Markets, all the time pretty much ignoring my family, the ones I love the most. Or was the business really where my love was?

Matthew 6:21 says, "Store up for yourselves treasures in heaven, where moth and rust do not destroy, and where thieves do not break in and steal. For where your treasure is, there your heart will be also." Our treasure is where we place our priorities.

With the wisdom that God had promised him, Solomon was able to make decisions that built "his" kingdom, and all the people prospered for it (or did they as they were taxed accordingly. Hum, sound familiar?). Other kings and nobles traveled countless miles to seek Solomon's wisdom, always bringing gold and precious items to show their appreciation. Hence, resulting in Solomon's wealth, estimated at about $2.1 trillion in today's values, obviously, to this day would be more than twice ever accumulated by a one individual.

Moral values

In the humanly, exulted, position that Solomon was in, and with the wisdom that God had given him, it gave him a pedestal to observe greed, hypocrisy, oppression, injustice, laziness, cursing, and jealousy as the standard moral among the people around him. Pondering these human traits, he came to the conclusion that

- Patience is better than pride,
- Envy is a driving force in human achievement,
- Bribery corrupts the heart,
- Anger takes up residence in the lap of fools.
- As there is righteousness, there is also wickedness, and the two will always be.
- No one knows whether love or hate awaits him. We do not know our future. We can only do the best that we can and have faith that Another is in control.
- We cannot live in this world without being bombarded by immoral values and human choices (however, that doesn't mean that we have to allow it to control how we choose to live).

Our fallen nature

God made mankind upright, but men have gone in search of many schemes. In other words, man's troubles are of his own devising, and these wicked schemes lead us from the good purposes of God.

As is quoted in verse 7:20, "There is not a righteous man on earth, who does what is right and *never* [italics added] sins." Although we were made in God's image, we (all) were born with a sinful nature although through God's help, we can fight back much of this nature. However, it will always be a continuing battle until the day we take our last breath. Then, and only then, we will be thrusted into eternal life of either eternal good or eternal evil.

Ultimate accountability

Through his God-given wisdom, Solomon determined:

> In the place of justice, wickedness was always there. (v. 3:16)

> I thought in my heart, God will bring to the judgement both the righteous and the wicked. (v. 3:17)

> Be happy, young man, while you are young... Follow the ways of your heart and whatever your eyes see, but know that for all these things, God will bring you to judgement. (v. 11:9)

Solomon or, as he portrays himself in scripture, The Preacher amasses his evidence in terms of creation, beauty, morality, meaning, justice, and our yearning for transcendence (translated by synonyms in the Merriam-Webster dictionary: distinction, dominance, eminence, noteworthiness, preeminence, preponderance, prepotency, prestigiousness, primacy, superiority, and supremacy; otherwise our individual selfishness, whether hidden or observed).

The Preacher starts Ecclesiastes by saying:

> Meaningless! Meaningless! Utterly meaningless! Everything is meaningless. What do people gain from all their labors at which they toil under the

sun? Generations come and generations go, but the earth remains forever. The sun rises and the sun sets, and hurries back to where it rises. The wind blows to the south and turns to the north; around and around it goes, ever returning on its course. All streams flow into the sea, yet the sea is never full. To the place the streams come from, there they return again. (1:1–7)

And he ends the book of Ecclesiastes by saying:

Remember your Creator in the days of your youth, before the days of trouble come and the years approach when you will say, "I find no pleasure in them"; before the sun and the light and the moon and the stars grow dark, and the clouds return after the rain; when the keepers of the house tremble, and the strong men stoop, when the grinders cease because they are few, and those looking through the widows grow dim; when the doors to the street are closed and the sound of grinding fades; when people rise up at the sound of birds, but all their songs grow faint; when people are afraid of heights and of dangers in the street; when the almond tree blossoms and the grasshopper drags itself along and desire no longer is stirred. Then people go to their eternal home and mourners go about the streets. Remember Him; before the silver cord is severed and the golden bowl is broken; before the pitcher is shattered at the spring and the wheel broken at the well, and the dust returns to the ground it came from, and the spirit returns to God who gave it. Meaningless! Meaningless! Says the Teacher. Everything is meaningless! (12:1–8)

Let me please translate these verses the best that I know how, although I am sure many don't need it.

- "Remember your Creator"—You were created by Him, and just like something that we build we own, we are God's property.
- "Before the days of trouble come"—when you are old and more feeble.
- "Before the sun and the light and the moon and the stars grow dark"—when your eyesight starts to weaken.
- "When the keepers of the house tremble"—for fear of his last days.
- "Strong men stoop"—Our back weakens, and we start to stoop over.
- "The grinders cease because they are few"—talking about our teeth.
- "The doors of the streets are closed"—Lips that used to say much will speak less.
- "The sound of the grinding fades"—Older people eat less because they need less.
- "Rise up at the at the songs of birds"—will rise earlier because the older sleep less.
- "All their songs grow faint"—because your hearing will weaken.
- "When people are afraid of heights"—Older folks are less stable and fall more.
- "The almond tree shall flourish"—Almond blossoms turn white as the hair on our head.
- "Grasshopper shall be a burden, and desire shall fail"—As we get older, we are more acceptable to disease, and with age, our sexual desires fail away.
- "Mourners go about the streets"—Funerals are more common in the life of the elderly.
- "The silver cord and the golden bowl are both speaking of death"—The water of life no longer flows.

Solomon ends highlighting all the wisdom that he has been given in summing up our lives like the waters in the rivers that go out to the sea only to return again. What is born of flesh is flesh. Flesh returns to dirt or nothing.

Then after all his years of wisdom and enjoying every possible "thing" in life, he ends with, "Now all has been heard; here is the conclusion of the matter: Fear God and keep his commandments, for this is the duty of all mankind. For God will bring every deed into judgement, including every hidden thing, whether it is good or evil" (12:13–14).

Reading and studying Ecclesiastics did not convince me that we should sell Glen's Markets, but I believe it had a subliminal impact on my thinking of what was really, really important in life. I had always felt a purpose in being in the grocery industry. I have visited many countries and read about many, many more whose, in order to obtain their daily food, people's lives are absorbed with that effort the majority of their days. Likewise, I remember seeing pictures of, so-called, grocery store shelves in Russia before communism was abolished. The shelves were 50%–60% empty of product (not uncommon in many countries), and like many countries today, the choice of variety is extremely limited. It gave me a proud feeling that we could offer over thirty-five thousand different products to our customers in each of our stores in northern and upper Michigan. We, and our suppliers, would bring products from all over the world and offer them every day for the benefit of need and convenience for our customers. We pride ourselves in quality and variety. It takes a constant, extreme network of effort in our food industry to accomplish this, one that is not, as I said, offered in most countries.

But while reading Ecclesiastes, I sensed a feeling of putting a can of beans on the shelf today only to have the need to replace that same product on that same shelf tomorrow, may not be what the Lord had in mind for me anymore. Well, perhaps, just perhaps, there might be more in this life that I was expected to be doing.

Did I personally decide to bail out of the grocery business? No! It never crossed my mind. I did start to realize that the crazy hours that I worked, about twice of those of my closest friends, may have been giving me personal satisfaction in my (selfish) ambitions, but it has been taking me away from those who I always said (and believed) were the most important things/people in my life.

About the same time, God (as He often does) seemed to continually put a verse in front of my eyes: Matthew 6:21, "For where your treasure is, there your heart will be also." Surely, my actions were not reflecting my heart, or perhaps, sadly were they?

I do believe that God did speak to me through the reading and study of Ecclesiastes, preparing my heart for the future of His will in my life. He has two ways that He communicates with us: through prayer and through reading/studying His inspired Word.

Summary

To sum things up, the process of getting us to the point where we considered and decided to sell a company that operated for over forty-eight years by three generations was as follows:

- Dad introduced that initial shocking thought he planted a buried seed.
- God led me to read and study His book of Ecclesiastes (subconsciously opening my mind to such a transaction).
- My business partner, Denny, chose to exit the business, walking away and retiring (although he didn't totally retire). Retiring had never crossed my mind. Dad sold out. I guess I figured that would be how I (or any family member) would exit. At fifty-three years of age, Denny left to become a full-time minister. Down deep, I know I really admired him for that!
- Different companies, large nationally known companies, kept inquiring about purchasing us. Although those inquiries continued to fall on deaf ears, it tickled our egos that they thought so highly of our company that they desired to absorb us into theirs. We certainly weren't in a weak financial condition; in fact, we were extremely solvent. It wasn't like we would be considered weak from a leadership

position; the opposite had been shared with us as to how the industry viewed us. Plus we had Glen B. as the third generation continually taking a larger part of the decision-making, convincing us of our great positioning for another generation.

- We had the threat of new competition. The A&P had disappeared from northern Michigan. The Kroger had come and gone over the years. Although there were a number of other independent operators, like ourselves, our team had always hit the competition head on, and we had persevered. The Walmart superstores posed a threat, but our confidence in our quality, service, cleanliness, and uniqueness gave us the confidence that we would survive. Meijer would be a challenge. We respected them, but again, although it would be tough, we felt we could persevere.

- I believe the wisdom of thought that my son Glen shared in my office that surprising day was perhaps the crack that got me to finally realize that having a family company for one hundred years was maybe not really the biggest priority in life to focus on.

Hence, Spartan Stores Inc. purchased

So often, our brains are like a sponge, and they soak up all that we hear. Other times, they are like a rock of ego, not allowing new options to penetrate. I would like to think that my brain is more like a huge funnel with a screen at the base. Just before the contents poured into it can journey to the narrow chamber below, they are blended toward a focused direction. Thus, all is fed into the larger top of the funnel, swirls around the tapering sides, and purifies itself until it gets to the final screening to be huddled together toward the focus of one result. That, in a simple description, is how I personally filtered the process that brought the Catt and Freeman Families to sell Glen's Markets. Truthfully, had my son never wanted to sell, it wouldn't have and couldn't have happened. I would have *never* allowed it!

Picture from the Michigan Food News, September 1986
as they announced a father & son transition team

Picture from the Michigan Food News, August 1997,
as they announced the father & son transition team

THE GLEN'S MARKET CULTURE

An Epilogue

There are so many things that we enjoyed, accomplished, and celebrated with our associates. I feel extremely guilty having to leave so many of their names out of this story, but like writing a documentary on your life with your family, if you are fortunate, there are just too many good things where you cannot pen them all to paper. If you are reading this as a past associate of Glen's Markets, and your name wasn't listed, please, please know you were not forgotten, and you too were appreciated, and I know you made a difference, a big difference!

Being part of a family business is just something that I am not able to put into words, like pursuing a Rocky Mountain elk with a bow and arrow or living with a couple of Eskimos in an unheated tent at thirty degrees below zero while you pursue musk ox in the Arctic (I tell these and other stories in my book, *Out There Somewhere*, published in 2020) or running, swimming, and biking a 32-mile triathlon (as Olympians do, but I never have). Unless you have experienced it, you are clueless as to what it entails. Nevertheless, words cannot express so much of what we feel.

There is the inside, ingrained, born-with feeling of ownership

There are the relational challenges between members of the family: dad with son and son with dad, and then in the next generation, dad with son and son with dad. Then you have other siblings involved in the business and those not involved in the business. At some time, along comes in-laws, etc., and the list can go on and on.

My father's and my relationship flourished after he retired and Denny/Sandy and I purchased the company. Realizing this, I strived to be more sensitive to the relationship I had with my children when they entered the business (as I don't question my father was too). However, perception is reality, and though I felt I was careful and tactful in the handling of my son(s), especially my oldest Glen B. (as Travis was becoming a shining star in our Information Technology Department because he is such a natural with computers; however, he was still fairly young when we sold the company), my feedback was that there were still barriers. Fortunately, our relationship has flourished since we sold the retail part of the company, and Glen has taken the lead of our commercial real estate (Travis and most recently Glen's son, Tanner, also help lead our commercial real estate).

As I have shared, early in my career, I was driven to make my dad proud. There were a few times when he would share those feelings (more often after he realized I was planning on leaving the company). But after we were able to purchase the company from him, he would walk into my office, like wanting to remind me, and he would tell me how proud he was with the direction the company was going, the team that we had built, and the results that we were getting. Perhaps the finest compliment that he ever gave me was when he said he realized that he had given birth to the company, but now it had outgrown him, and he was glad I was in control because he felt it was beyond his abilities. I don't know if I shared my thoughts with him at the time as I questioned the second half of his compliment, but also the thought I had was being glad that he gave birth to it as I really felt those sacrifices were something that I couldn't have accomplished. It's funny though as we handed the operations over to Glen B., I had the same feelings as my dad, Glen B. was more in position to take the company to the next level. He had earned it.

To say I was looking forward to the next-generation operating Glen's Markets would be an understatement. Glen B. had acquired the experience and proved himself where I knew the company could only blossom under his leadership. Had he not come in my office that day to share that, looking into the future, but had shared that he didn't want to sell and wanted to take the company into a successive generation, there is no way I could have or would have signed those papers to sell Glen's Markets. Family is important. *"If you ain't been there, you just don't know where there is.*

Thank you for visiting the Glen's Market history of culture. May God bless you in each and every one of your endeavors as you seek His wisdom and direction.

Final note: There are literally thousands upon thousands of associates who have been the backbone in the success of Glen's Markets over its forty-eight years—1951–1999. It is unfortunate that I could not name many more in this book as many of us, who are named and pictured, could only hold our positions because of the thousands that aren't named but are affectionately remembered. To each of you, I wish to say *thank you* for making Glen's Markets the institution that it was!

Quoting my last "Food for Thought" message that was posted in our printed advertising:

> Let it never be forgotten that glamour is not greatness; applause is not fame; prominence is not eminence. The man of the hour is not apt to be the man of the ages. A stone may sparkle, but that does not make it a diamond; people may have money, but that does not make them a success.
>
> It is what the unimportant people do that really counts and determines the course of history. The greatest forces in the universe are never spectacular. Summer showers are more effective than hurricanes, but they get no publicity. The world would soon die but for the fidelity, loyalty, and consecration of those whose names are unhonored and unsung.

Blessings...live life intentionally!

Glen

ABOUT THE AUTHOR

Glen A. Catt was born in Paw Paw, Michigan, a town where his father, C. Glen Catt, was currently the store manager of a Kroger grocery store. Growing up in Gaylord, Michigan, as part of a small family business, Glen actually started working in his father's store when he was five years old. At twelve, he became the number one bagger (only because if he was there, he was the first one they would call to bag groceries). At fifteen, he was taught to run a cash register. Throughout high school, Glen kept a twenty to twenty-five hour schedule at the store, only experiencing Friday night sporting games and dances after the store would close.

By the time he was transferred to his father's Kalkaska store, Glen had managed or worked every department in the store including the meat department (with knife scars to prove it). After nine years as a store manager, three years as a district manager, and another five years as the company operations manager, Glen and his brother-in-law (and sister) bought the then fourteen stores with seven hundred associates from their father. At the sale of the retail arm of the company, Glen's Markets had grown to twenty-four supermarkets, two limited assortment stores, upwards of 2,500 associates, and an annual volume of $265 million in sales.

With their four children grown and married, blessing them with seven grandchildren, Glen and Jeanne spend their time between their home in Gaylord, Michigan, and their second home in Livingston, Montana. Glen is an avid hunter as displayed in his previous book, *Out There Somewhere: One Man's Quest for Hunting Adventures*, which shares stories and pictures of numerous of his hunting adventures around North American and Africa. He also continues to be active in his church and various ministries that promote the gospel of Jesus Christ.

9 781636 305745